MW00453283

May 2011

Marilee Cash

July 2017
Dot Shipp
Aug 2017

Faith Through Aging Eyes

Copyright ©2014 by Roselyn Aronson Staples
All Rights Reserved

ISBN: 9780692409466

CONTENTS

DEDICATION

This book is dedicated to my friend, Jean Raver.

OREWORD

FAITH THROUGH AGING EYES

As a relatively "young" person assigned to ministry with senior adults, I deliberately chose to use the word "we" when addressing "our" group. Over the years, awareness gradually dawned: aging people look old to other people but they don't feel old themselves. But wait, could this mean that I have drifted into this dreaded category known as a "senior?" My birth date would indicate "yes," but do I really need a geriatric doctor? Do I qualify for senior discounts?

As I battled with this reality, I recognized in my peers a spiritual vitality that did not diminish with the decline of physical strength and mental acuity.

It was when my mother, in the later years of dementia, was unable to recognize time or place but able to teach on the resurrection of Jesus that I was impacted by a profound truth. Our spirits do not get old or sick. His Power is made perfect in weakness, even if that weakness is due to aging.

A sense of excitement began to override my resistance to

aging. From a spiritual perspective, my strongest days are ahead of me. Now, at age 71, my adventure with God is just beginning. So this book, Faith through Aging Eyes, is filled with stories of watching God be God through the lenses of living in a body with more history than future.

I welcome you to join me on this journey as we celebrate the precious gift of experiencing Faith Through Aging Eyes.

ACKNOWLEDGEMENTS

This book has been written from my encounters with life. You will recognize yourself in many of the stories, and as you do, remember I am grateful to you.

Beverly Rehfeld, you have been a gift as an editor. Your gentle strength has guided me as I have clarified and rewritten content. Your authentic heart has transformed sentences in my own soul that needed editing.

Jean Raver, your journey with me has been the longest and the deepest. Thank you for making my practical needs your ministry so that I could have mine. Thank you for opening my eyes to the world of art and adventure. Thank you for inviting me to embrace faith through iconoclastic glasses.

Stuart Briscoe, thank you for trusting me with a position on your pastoral team.

Jean Roesler, thank you for serving alongside me as a ministry partner.

As I sort through memories, I remember our Kid's Kamp Staff, Senior Adult Ministry, and Prayer Team Leadership.

I think of friends whose stories have shaped mine. There is no way I can list all of you, but you know who you are.

Virgil, I thank you for your prayers and generosity.

Papa God, Jesus, and Holy Spirit, thank you for revealing to me that you are the object of Faith Through Aging Eyes.

An Unspeakable Gift

As a community health nurse, it was my responsibility to meet with hospitalized patients to arrange follow-up home care. One afternoon I met with a client of mine who was only 34 years old. I had read her hospital chart and knew that she had cancer of the throat. The doctor's notes indicated that her life expectancy was only a few months and social services had recorded that she had five small children at home.

Surgery had robbed her of the ability to speak, so I allowed extra time for my interview. I would need to ask her questions and give her a small whiteboard so she could write her answers. I introduced myself to this young woman, whose name was Mary, and explained my purpose for being there. Her face was still heavily bandaged because of the extensive surgery she had just come through. When I asked my first question and handed her the whiteboard, tears began to run down her cheeks.

I pondered what had prompted this look of fear and sadness. Then, hoping that I was wrong, I said, "Mary, you can't read." Her posture confirmed this dreaded explanation. With a sinking realization that this dying mother would never be able to tell anyone how she felt, I quietly asked God, "What am I going to do?" His answer was immediate. "Teach her to talk to me." I put my assessment materials aside, leaned closer to Mary's face and said, "Mary, I am going to teach you to pray." And that is what I did.

I am so thankful for the teaching of Psalm 39 that assures us that before the word is on our tongue, God knows it completely. Mary could "talk" freely to God without voice or literacy. Of course, we made arrangements for her other needs as well, using posters and pictures. Mary soon returned home, leaving me to wonder how things were going.

A couple of months later, I "happened" to be in the emergency room when an ambulance pulled up and a patient was wheeled in by cart. I immediately recognized Mary. My heart was pounding as I leaned over her and eagerly asked, "Mary, has God been real to you?" Mary's eyes shone as she lifted her hand from the blanket to show me a thumbs up.

When have you been unspeakably thankful for the gift of prayer?

*D*ON'T LOOK AT YOUR FEET

I have been over thinking for a couple of days. I have some decisions to make, some plans to present, and some options to consider. It's hard to maintain eye contact with Jesus when you are distracted by that which you are stumbling over.

I am reminded of a time when I was a guest at a wedding reception. The father of the bride was a ballroom dance instructor. His performance on the dance floor was stunning. All eyes were on him as he and his new bride daughter floated across the dance floor.

Later in the evening, the magic moment occurred. This father came up to me and asked me to dance. Honored, I walked with him to the dance floor. As the music started, my eyes immediately fell to my feet. At the same moment, I felt the palm of my partner's hand lifting my chin. His words, "Nobody looks at their feet when they dance with me. It's my job to make you look good." His strong hand on my back and his confidence made me both look and feel like a dancer. I remember thinking, "This is fun."

I wonder if Jesus wants to lift my chin today. I wonder if

He wants to posture my face in such a way that my eyes will focus on Him. He is fully aware of that which I am prone to stumble over. He's attentive to it but not concerned.

I think He wants me to hear Him saying, "Don't look at your feet when you're dancing with Me."

*T*HE COMFORT OF AN ADVOCATE

I had a month of legal and logistical pressure. I found myself in places of tension with city ordinances, building inspectors, insurance adjustors, real estate offers, amendments, banking legislations, and the list goes on.

It was a month of placing phone calls received by a machine that doesn't return calls, trying to decide which menu number will connect me with a person rather than more scripted computer options. All of this had left me with feelings of abandonment.

But then I encountered an advocate. He not only carefully listened to my concerns, but he calmly and competently lifted the load from my shoulders and transferred it to his. His relaxed mannerisms and his verbal communication assured me that this load was not heavy for him. There would be no financial cost to me. He actually thanked me for allowing him to take on my burden.

In John's first letter, chapter two, he assures us that we have an advocate with the Father. I am thankful today for a picture of this advocate. I thank God for the people in my life who are a reflection of Jesus.

$\mathscr{T}$IME HEALS

I am familiar with the phrase "time heals" when applied to an ache or pain. Sometimes time is the best medicine. I recently watched as time was the basket in which a different type of healing was delivered. Here is the story.

A person who had suffered much from physical pain, emotional agony, spiritual darkness, and relational disappointment agreed to accept a visit from yet another Christian. But there was something different about this visit. Instead of leaving a trail of more empty promises and unfounded advice, this visitor is remembered as someone who would be welcome to come again. In fact, there is hope that she will come again.

How was she different? I could honestly say she was authentic, nonjudgmental, a good listener, compassionate and fun. With all of this being true, if I had to pick one characteristic as the critical game changer, I would acknowledge another attribute.

I would say she was all of the above framed in the gift of time. She did not make an appointment. She did not check her watch. She came and stayed. When we all got tired, she asked what time it was. Her husband had even called her to see if she was all right as it had grown quite late.

Does time unmeasured and freely given express love that heals? I believe it does!

HEARTBREAK OVERSHADOWS REASON

We were the only ones in the boutique.

My friend, who loves to create a wardrobe for me that goes far beyond what I would choose for myself, was on a roll. I knew from experience that we were in familiar territory. My friend tries to convince me that I need to update my clothes. I respond by saying I think what I have is fine. She then tells me I can't have the job I have and look like I look. She chooses thirty new things for me. I continue to resist but in the end buy ten. I then leave them in my closet for about a month.

One day I take a risk and wear one of them. I am quickly surrounded by people who love what I am wearing. I have even been identified as someone who is into fashion, and unless I tell the story above, that is the impression I give.

Yesterday had a new twist. Only one person staffed this small, artistic boutique. I had called the day before and learned they were open from 9 am to 3 pm. We arrived at the shop just a little after 2 pm. About a half hour into our shopping excursion, the attendant began looking at her watch, asking if there were any articles of clothing she could return to the racks.

I was frantically trying on new things and negotiating with my friend, and at one point even told the sales attendant she should give my friend a commission. At 3 pm we were checking out. I had a stack of new clothes that I knew I would eventually come to love.

The sales attendant started adding up the cost, trying to calculate sale items and giving credit where appropriate. When my friend handed her the credit card, the attendant announced a price that was less than half of what we expected. When we asked if she was sure she had charged us for everything, the attendant realized she had two pages of receipt records but had only charged us for one.

After she finished the second calculation, my friend asked her if she had charged us for a piece of jewelry. The sales lady said "No" and ran the charge again. As she was doing this, my friend noticed a pair of harem pants she thought would be perfect for me. She convinced me to try them on, and we added them to the checkout pile.

The sales lady sighed impatiently and said the store had been closed for a half hour. I responded by telling her I had called a day prior and been informed the store was open until 3 pm. The lady then asked me what time it was. I told her it was 3:01 pm.

Confused by her reluctance to take our business, I asked, "Aren't you happy to make a sale?" I silently wondered why she wouldn't be as no one else was shopping in the store. It was then that she told me she was very happy to make the sale but had just placed her husband in a nursing home, and she was anxious to go and see him. She explained he had advanced Alzheimer's.

I asked if he knew her. She said, "Yes, and he also knows I am the one who put him in there." She said she had taken him home five times.

Sometimes adding sales receipts, making a profit, attending to customers, and being cordial are all superficial intrusions into the terror and heartbreak of real life.

JOLTED BY GRACE

What happened? I was backing out of our garage as I
usually do. There is no need to pay careful attention to that
which you do routinely. But this morning the car jolted to
a sudden stop for no reason at all.

Stunned, I tried to discern what had stopped the car's
momentum. It was then that my eyes caught both the rear
view mirror and the side mirror. I had been backing up
against the big, white van of our houseguest. I wondered
why I hadn't heard the crash or the sound of metal crushing
metal.

Trembling, I opened the car door and walked back to
check the damage. What I saw was a 2-inch space between
my back bumper and the van. What (or Who) intervened
in my careless behavior? Who, besides me, had control of
my car?

I sat for a few minutes and pondered this incident. Had I
caught God in the act of grace? How often has He
protected me when I have not noticed?

As I resumed my drive into work, I found myself settling
into two postures. I was on red alert to what might be in

my path AND I was resting in the safety of having a Protector.

Have you ever been jolted by grace?

WHEN DYING IS THE NEXT STEP

We live in a time where dying is complex. There are so many options and so many decisions. As a child, I remember that when people's bodies stopped working, they died at home. It was an expectation for those who were old and sick. Today, we somehow feel we need to prevent it.

I wonder if we have forgotten that God has reserved for Himself the decision for life to begin and life to end. If we believe this, we are quick to say that we do not have the right to end the life of the unborn, but we must also acknowledge that we do not have the right to deny death.

I was asked this week to help a family whose physician had asked if they wanted to insert a feeding tube into a 96-year-old lady who could no longer swallow. I responded by saying that interfering with death is as wrong as interfering with life.

I say this with confidence because I know that if God was not ready to take this person home, He would give her the ability to swallow. We do not have as much power in these stories as we fear.

This story is also a reminder that Jesus took care of our

death, but He left the dying to us. Dying is a grueling task that is only softened by the promise of eternal life.

Let us live by the power of the risen Christ and die with the peace of knowing this is the next step in His preordained plan of amazing grace.

*B*ENT BUT NOT BROKEN!

For the past few days, I have been watching a tree in our backyard whose branches are covered with snow. One of the branches draws my attention as it is not able to support the weight of the snow. Leaving its usual inconspicuous spot as part of the tree, it has arched backward, its tip on the ground.

I wonder why that branch is not able to support the weight of the snow when all the other branches can.

Is it broken? Do we need a chainsaw? (Or is it patience that we need?)

After a few days of warm sunshine, the branch snapped back to its usual place. It has been restored and is now indistinguishable from the other branches.

It was burdened with snow. The burden was melted by the warm sun, and it is now free to grow.

This is particularly interesting to me as I have set the morning aside to seek God's help in releasing grief and emotional burden to Him. How can I learn from the restored branch?

- Is there something in me that takes on more weight than I can support?

- Do I cling to it too long before releasing it to Jesus?

- Do I welcome angel wings to come and brush the burden away?

- Do I trust the God of consuming fire to melt my grief without destroying me?

- Will I invite the breath of the Holy Spirit to set me free?

- Do I trust that I am secure in the trunk of the tree and, therefore, will be restored?

Yes, because I am only bent, not broken!

WHAT MOVIE IS JESUS WATCHING?

A note from a missionary friend has stirred my heart. This is the true story of a return flight from the US to the field where my friend serves.

"A woman from the country to which I was returning was thrilled when I sat down next to her on the plane. She was 71 years old and very nervous about the flight. When I spoke her language to her, she started kissing me. I think that I got at least a dozen kisses on that flight. It was a bit like sitting next to a young child though. She did not know how to fasten her seat belt or how to open containers on her food tray. When I asked her if she wanted to watch a movie, she said that she would rather lay her head on my shoulder and just look at a movie on my screen. I had to smile affectionately at her."

I love the picture this story invites me to imagine. I love to let myself feel this deeply as both of these women received God's love with skin.

I want to hear God speak to me in my language. I want to lean my head on to His shoulder and watch the movie He is watching today.

I know He sees things with the confidence that "It is Finished!" I know He sees the battle as Won! I know He looks at me with compassion when I tremble because the battle I am in today is fierce. I am glad that God knows that at the age of 71, I need Him to care for me with the tenderness of a parent.

I don't want to watch my movie today. I want to lean on His shoulder and watch His.

AM I DRAGGING MY RAM?

The story of Abraham is one that never fails to challenge me. This man trusted God so completely that he was willing to sacrifice his son, Isaac. How can any parent be asked to give their son as a sacrifice? And in this case, how can the very God who made the promise seemingly be the one to sabotage it?

I have learned that Abraham and Isaac are a picture of God the Father and His only Son, our Lord Jesus Christ. I have learned that Abraham's obedience is a type of testing of faith and it was credited to him as righteousness.

I know that God is a jealous God, and He insists on my trust. This means He may ask me to sacrifice that which is most precious to me. Sometimes I am able to start the journey up the mountain in order to demonstrate my absolute surrender. I find, though, that I often get very tired as I travel. I wonder if I am dragging my own ram just in case God doesn't show up.

We do this every time we sing "I Surrender All," but even as we are singing, we are withholding enough to keep ourselves safe in case God doesn't "show up."

19

COME, SEE A MIRACLE

I grew up on a farm and on a routine day after our evening meal, my dad and mom would go out to the barn for a couple of hours to milk the cows, provide feed and water for the animals, and check on the various gerrymandered creations that kept broken- down equipment last past their normal expiration date so that our basic needs could be met.

It was on one of these evenings that my mother arrived at the door of our house and breathlessly said, "Honey, get your coat. I want to show you a miracle." She helped me with my thick, hand-me-down, altered-to-fit coat and tied a scarf around my head.

We walked to the barn with the winter snow crunching beneath our feet. (I still miss those nights when the air was clear, the stars were bright, and the snow crunched with each step.) When we reached the barn, the familiar smell of animals and the warmth their bodies emitted felt comforting to me.

Mom was undistracted in her mission to show me this miracle. She took me to the platform behind the stanchions where the cows were secured. (This is where I had learned to be careful because a cow's tail can be a memorable whip.)

We stopped where Dad was standing behind a cow. He had a long rope that seemed secured under the cow's tail and was pulling with all of his might. Mom's non-verbal posture compelled me to be quiet and watch.

Before long, the feet of a calf, tied by the rope, came forth from under the cow's tail as my dad continued to pull. Then, at a speed almost too fast for words, the calf's head appeared and the whole body slipped to the clean straw below. The calf had barely landed when it rose with shaky legs to its feet. Somehow, even though secured in a stanchion, the mother was able to crane her neck and push the calf up to her face, removing any film that would inhibit the calf from breathing clearly. She then used her rather strong neck movements to push the calf to her udder where he quickly found the perfect anatomical protrusions to fill his mouth and begin a rhythmical sucking of milk.

I am so grateful for the gift of growing up on a farm and for a mother who recognized miracles.

I wonder why, when I worked as a nurse, I cried every time I saw a baby born.

What have you learned from a life experience that still fills your heart with wonder?

*P*UTTING GRANDMA IN THE GRAVE

(Written for a family who asked me to craft a Service of Committal that would help their grandchildren understand the process and purpose of this service.)

There is no way to make what we are going to do here easy. As we actually put the body that your grandmother used to live in into the grave, we feel all kinds of things. There is something basically wrong about this. And God understands these feelings better than we do. Our feelings of sadness feel like fear and sometimes it all feels like confusion. That's because death is both an enemy and friend.

It is an enemy because it robs us of the time we would have with someone we love. God doesn't like it either. We would not have sickness and death if we didn't have sin. Death is an enemy BUT it is an enemy that God defeated when Jesus rose again from the dead. Our bodies will die, but when they do, if we belong to Jesus, He comes to get us and we don't die at all. We just move to where He is and wait with Him for the rest of the family. Actually, the person who goes to Heaven doesn't wait at all because there is no time there. It is only those of us left here on earth who wait. And finally, at the end of everything here on earth, the Bible says we all get new bodies. I'm still not sure how that works.

Death is also a friend because when we have lived on this earth for as long as God thinks it is a good idea, death frees us from this body that the Bible calls a tent. This is what happened to your grandmother, and what we are going to do now is place her tent in the grave because she doesn't need it anymore. Your grandmother isn't here at the cemetery today. She's already gone on ahead to be with Jesus. But we don't throw her body just anywhere because it is the thing that she lived in and we want to show respect for it. This place will have a marker with her name on it. It will be a place where you can visit if you want to, remembering the special times you have had together.

Sometimes it might feel to you like Grandmother is actually talking to you when you remember things she said to you. That will be the Holy Spirit, reminding you of the truth she taught you. The Bible tells us not to talk to the dead but the Holy Spirit loves to remind us of truth. And if you want to say something to her, you can ask Jesus to tell her.

In 2 Timothy 1:5-6, Paul reminds Timothy that he sincerely trusts the Lord because he has the faith of his mother and of his grandmother. He then tells him to fan into flame the spiritual gift God gave him. My prayer for you is that you will hang on tight to the faith of your grandmother and live life as she did.

Because God, who is in charge of everything, has called your grandmother home to Himself, we now commit the body she used to live in to the earth. And we commit her into the hands of her loving heavenly Father and our Lord and Savior Jesus Christ who said, "I am going ahead to get a room ready for you."

STEEP STEPS AND CRUTCHES

The church begged to be photographed. It is a classic white structure with a steeple that points through the towering pines to the heavens.

At the time of my childhood, which is the setting for these memories, the front door of the church was accessed by a long flight of narrow steep steps. It was a nightmare for a man on crutches. It could have been a valid reason not to attend.

But not for my grandpa. For him and for us it only meant we left early for church so he would have the time to do the agonizing work of climbing those steps with crutches.

As a child, I hated to wait as Grandpa struggled with this weekly climb. Today I cherish this picture as a stepping-stone for my own faith.

Something was compelling Grandpa. No, not something. Someone! Thank you, Jesus.

Who put stepping-stones in your childhood faith?

*L*ESSONS FROM A TATTOO

I met her in the hospital. She was a patient who was assigned to me for her admission work-up. I was a recent graduate nurse and was learning from each new patient, but from this one I learned a lesson that helped to shape my life.

She was an elderly lady and by first impression it seemed she had lived a hard life. There were no masks of make up or hair color treatments. Her clothes were ragged and old. They may have fit at one time but now they were bigger than her thin frame needed. Her wrinkled skin looked like she had spent a lot of time in the sun.

A hospital admission procedure by a nurse involves asking many questions about presenting problems and assembling a health history. Next a physical examination is done, looking for signs and symptoms that will help in establishing a preliminary diagnosis. As I was checking her skin, I noticed the markings of an old tattoo on her forearm. I didn't want to be biased but couldn't escape the thought that she did not in any way fit into my category of someone who would get a tattoo. I asked her to tell me about it and sat in rapt attention as she told me her story.

It happened during the Depression. Her mother had died when she and her brother were around three years old. Her father was unable to find work in the Texas area where they lived and as a last resort agreed to take an assignment with the Coast Guard. This meant that her brokenhearted father had to place his two children in an orphanage. Upon learning that he would be out at sea for at least six months and fearing that his children would get lost in the system, mixed up with other kids, or he not have the right paperwork to reclaim them, he did a profound thing. He had his name tattooed on their arms so that no one could ever question who these children belonged to.

My heart was flooded with compassion and respect for this father. Then I was reminded of how like our Heavenly Father he was. Isaiah 49:16 quotes the Lord, "See, I have engraved you on the palms of My hands." I don't think my patient was given a path in life that was easy to walk. I do think she could look at her arm and know she had a father who loved her.

So many times when my faith has worn thin, I have comforted myself with the assurance that my heavenly Father has carved my name on His hand. Do you have that comfort today?

CAN THIS MACHINE RUN?

Can you make this machine run? A friend advised me that a snow blower that I am trying to keep running might be beyond repair. "It is cheaply made," he explained. I was surprised to hear this discouraging report because the paint is still shiny. It is only being used for a second year, but getting it started and keeping it running has made me hope it doesn't snow. But is it really hopeless?

Before I made funeral arrangements for this snow blower, I decided to ask another friend for his opinion. His answer was immediate. "Of course it can run. All an engine needs to run is fuel, compression, and spark." I was intrigued with this second opinion and eager to learn from this innovative artist for whom anything is possible. He taught me about the carburetor, and I watched as every part was cleaned, installed, and checked. When he was satisfied everything was in place, he pulled the cord to the manual start and the machine roared to life.

I went home and looked up the definitions for fuel, compression, and spark, and this is what I found. Fuel is any material that stores energy that can later be extracted to perform mechanical work in a controlled manner. Compression is force that tends to shorten or squeeze something, decreasing its volume. The term spark ignition is used to describe the system with which the air–fuel mixture inside the combustion chamber of an internal combustion engine is ignited by a spark. The resulting controlled explosion delivers the power to turn the reciprocating mass inside the engine.

Considering all of this leads me to ponder the work of the Holy Spirit in my life. The Spirit fills me with energy that can be released through me in His time. That with which He fills me in the morning is compressed by the experiences of the day He ordains so that when the energy is released, it has increased in power but decreased in volume. (Especially when it refers to my talking.) And finally, the Holy Spirit is the spark that prompts action and delivers power.

Time will tell which mechanic's appraisal of this snow blower was correct, but I am grateful for the mechanical lesson that has provided me with an analogy of how the Holy Spirit works in my life.

Lord, produce a controlled explosion in and through me today.

*J*OY AND PAIN

I remember wondering if there would be a way to write joy and pain in the same space. It was important to me because I was teaching a course called "Love that Heals." We were learning about suffering and exploring how joy can be embraced even when pain is unrelenting.

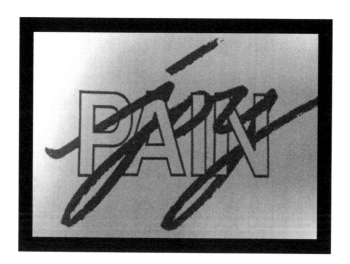

I called our graphic artist and asked her to write joy and pain in the same space. The logo above is what she produced for me. I have used it extensively for the past 25 years.

There came a day when this artist stepped back into my life

and asked me to pray with her. As I listened to her, I heard a heartbreaking personal story. Though her eyes were moist, she broke into a hearty laugh that was easily recognizable as hers. I realized this friend not only created this graphic but was living it. She messaged me a few days later and said, "By God's amazing grace, my trust in Him is as strong and sure as it has ever been, so indeed 'It is Well with My Soul.'"

I was reading about how David stood up to the Giant with just five smooth stones and a stick, and one BIG, HUGE GOD on his side. So there! Because of His Word, I am choosing to see things from a place of victory. Let's watch and learn what God will do!

How does *Faith Through Aging Eyes* create a space for both joy and pain?

GOD, WHERE DO YOU WANT ME TO BE?

This question had become a familiar prayer for me over a certain period of time. I had somehow decided that there were three essential places that I needed to be...all at the same time. My prayer for God to speak to me was genuine and I intended to follow the guidance I was seeking.

What I didn't have on the checklist that I had prepared for God was the answer He gave me one morning. I believe God said, "Your presence is not critical to any of those three places. I have them under My control. Actually," He continued, "I have prepared these three environments as gifts for you. Each of them will reveal more of who I AM and be useful in molding you into my image."

There is a wonderful freedom in not being needed and a simultaneous joy in being wanted.

WHAT TO SAY WHEN THERE'S NOTHING TO SAY

I received an email from a friend who is experiencing life-altering medical symptoms and getting no clarity from a team of medical experts.

This is my response in part:

> First of all, thank you for trusting me with your cry for help. Tomorrow is my birthday, and I am aware that I have had an expectation that I would reach a time in life when my cries for help would be filled with less anguish and the list of answers would be longer than the list of questions, but neither is true.
>
> This much seems true to me today. We need each other for this journey of faith that is crammed with landmines. My husband's brother was a Marine who was especially trained to deactivate landmines. Only the Holy Spirit can deactivate that which our common enemy has planned for our demise. The victory of the cross is our only hope.
>
> I will walk with you on this journey, and I know you will walk with me. If, in the mysterious administration of God, He is calling you to weakness then trust that His

power will be amplified in it.

I will continue to pray for healing for you and for wisdom in knowing how to approach and respond to the complexities of our healthcare system.

Thank you that in the past when I have come to you with a broken heart, you have always led me to rest in the goodness of God. Today, my friend, I ask for the grace to be an echo of your wisdom and from the mountain you will hear, "Be still and know that I am God." Love and Peace to you.

What do you say when there is nothing to say?

$\mathcal{I}$ DIDN'T KNOW WE WERE POOR

I recently had a long conversation with a childhood friend. Her reflections on her growing-up years reminded me that I knew back then what I still know now. Her family was poor. They lived in a house without paint or plumbing. I wonder what justice would have looked like then. In hindsight I am sorry that we didn't share more of what we had, but at the time it seemed that we needed it all.

In addition to lifelong financial stress, this family has had more than its share of illness and death. Even today her medical history fills pages while mine is almost blank.

How is this fair?

But an even more perplexing question is why does she laugh more than I do?

When asked directly, my friend acknowledges that a "glass half full" attitude is not always easy to maintain. But, she adds, her mother was somehow able to do it.

"We had a wonderful childhood," she said. "I would not have been able to tell you we were poor because I didn't know it. I knew we ate a lot of potatoes, but for me everything was just fun."

I am left with two deeply personal questions. The first is this: Now that I have more than I need, what do I give to her? The second is this: How and what do I receive from her?

Do I know that I am poor?

A GOOD NAME

I have been asked to speak to a Senior Adult Fellowship on the topic "A Good Name." It is never easy for me to prepare a talk when the subject is chosen for me. The idea of "a good name" has been stirring in my mind since I accepted this invitation. Times when a name has had significance have been brought back to memory.

I grew up on a farm a few miles away from a village of less than 1,000 people where everybody knew everybody. During my college years, I came home whenever I could. On one such occasion, I noticed the variety store on Main Street was under new ownership. I shopped there for a few things and wrote a check for payment. I handed the check to the new owner and asked if he wanted to see identification. He looked at my check and smiled. Then he said the words that filled my heart with gratitude and pride, "Not with THAT name."

The name was recognized as one where trust had been earned. Dad's word was as good as a notarized document. This heritage has been prescriptive for me. After my parents' death, I was driven to sell their house the way Dad would have done it: with a handshake.

There is something about growing up with a name that is trusted that has given me confidence. It has shaped my identity. But does this name really define who I am?

As I prepare this message, I want to find ways to help the aged understand who they are as children of God, as joint heirs with Christ. In order to do this with authenticity, I need to answer the question for myself. Who am I?

Do I understand who I am because my Father's name is I AM?

Do I claim my inheritance as a joint heir with Christ?

Do I celebrate belonging to the family of God?

Do I assume a posture of power when the enemy whispers to me that I will be defeated?

Do I answer the enemy by saying: "Not with that Name!"

*D*O I REST OR RISK?

I want my body to be strong. I want the physical ability to do the things my heart longs to do. I don't want to hurt myself every time I lift something. I don't want to fall and break a bone.

Yesterday I met with a personal trainer. She assessed my strength. I couldn't even do one push up. My body doesn't have enough joints to follow the patterns she demonstrated for my test.

As I struggled through this assessment, she wrote many notes. I asked her if she had ever worked with anyone in such bad shape. She said my strength level was quite typical for someone in "my age group." She assured me that I will do well as she personalizes a torture chamber for me (the word "torture" is my term, not hers).

My body is telling me this morning that it would be happier if I would just let it rest. My heart is surging with a passion to push through the pain.

Do I rest or risk?

DREAD NO MORE

A common phrase that is used as an attempt to comfort someone is "waiting is the hardest place to be." There are some who will actually say that bad news is easier to deal with than no news.

Aging opens up opportunity for dread. Will I be able to do the activities of daily living? What if I end up alone with no one to call? What if I run out of money? What if my memory fails?

Faith responds by declaring there is nothing to fear. This is an easy statement to make but embracing it as experience requires trust. It means that I say "Amen" to the promises of God. It also means that I carefully discern what these promises are.

Where does this leave us with our practical challenges? Do we pray with the man who said to Jesus, "Lord, I believe, help my unbelief"?

A few years ago I had an experience that has potential to disempower dread. I was subject to a search by police in a country where Christian teaching by Westerners is illegal. The police believed I was breaking this law.

Because the protocol for justice in that environment was not trusted, the decision was made to hide me. The police were persistent in their search and were closing in on my hiding place. My heart was pounding so hard that I thought it wouldn't matter if I were captured as I felt I would die from fear anyway. At the very moment that I was discovered, I was suddenly filled with a sense of relief.

Once I was released and in a safe country, I began to reflect on my experience and wrote in my journal, "That which I dreaded I need dread no more for it was now a reality." Please don't take this to mean that all of your fears will be realized, but rather borrow the wisdom of Corrie Ten Boom who said, "You'll get the ticket when the train comes."

Most of the things we dread will never happen. Those that do will be accompanied by the power to respond to them in ways that make you wonder why you gave fear so much space in your life in the first place.

I invite you to benefit from my experience. "That which I dreaded I need dread no more for it was now a reality," and with that reality came absolute empowerment.

Let's honor God's promises by saying "Thank You" today for what we trust Him to do tomorrow.

A LITTLE BOAT IN CONSTANT READINESS

"...a vast multitude, hearing all the many things that He was doing, came to Him. And He told His disciples to have a little boat in [constant] readiness for Him because of the crowd, lest they press hard upon Him and crush Him."

These words, from Mark 3 (Amplified) appear to describe the preparation Jesus made for self-protection and preservation.

At other times, we see Jesus simply walking through an angry crowd and going on His way. (Luke 4:30)

It is beyond the scope of this book to talk about when and why Jesus accessed supernatural power, thus taking Him out of the scope of natural danger. For today, I want to think about why we might need "a little boat in constant readiness" and how we might secure one.

The "crowds" that threaten me are my thoughts, my memories, and my fears. Added to these are feelings of helplessness, conflicting schedules, and heartbreaking stories. I need to keep three boats within easy reach so that I am not crushed.

The first is the embrace of His Presence. By keeping my eyes focused on the face of Jesus and my ears tuned to the voice of the Holy Spirit, I have a refuge.

The second is the promise of God. I need to search His Word and find a promise that applies to my "crowd." If I don't know what promise to claim, I can ask the Holy Spirit to lead me to one. Then I can "remind" God that this is what He said. We can "Stand on the Promises" as the old hymn says. It is best if we get a grip on one promise that specifically applies and then storm heaven with it.

The third boat is people who will pray. A pop up just came up on my computer screen. It says, "You are now running on reserve battery power." That happened to me this morning, both emotionally and spiritually. I immediately emailed five friends who are interceding for me today.

I am glad Jesus gave us the picture of having a boat in constant readiness. Let's check both the availability and condition of our boats. The crowds will keep pressing but we have access to protection.

What boats do you have ready?

NEARSIGHTED FAITH

In the book of second Peter, we are reminded to not be nearsighted. Peter is talking about qualities that will keep us from being ineffective and unproductive in our knowledge of our Lord Jesus Christ.

If your eye doctor diagnoses you as nearsighted, it means that you are not able to see things far away. You can easily read a book that you are holding on your lap, but as you look into the distance, things become blurred.

How does this work for us who have more history than future? Is there a danger that we may be nearsighted as we look into the rearview mirror of our life?

One of the advantages to aging is the opportunity to recognize that what at first seems like a new encounter with God is actually the next chapter in a story that began years ago. God, whom Francis Thompson describes as the "Hound of Heaven," has been in pursuit of us throughout the story of our lives.

Let's ask the Holy Spirit to give us lenses that will enable us to recognize the encounters we have had with Him that are being used to create the story being woven today. Let's ask

Him to remind us of the prayers we prayed years ago that we are living in the good of today. Let's remember that the ministry we are called to is one that we have been prepared for through the environments we have been led.

God, let me not be nearsighted as I look into the rearview mirror of my life. May I walk in authority today as I am reminded that you are a promise-keeping God.

*S*HREDDING MY DATA

I have filled three huge lawn bags with shredded paper today. Hidden among the shreds are the details of my life.

I could tell you how much my electric bill was in 1980 if I had spared those receipts from the shredder. I could have assured you that my cat was vaccinated for rabies back in 1983. Or maybe you would be more interested in a document stating my car passed the emission test in 1990.

As I fed these things into the ravenous shredder, which has overheated three times, I wondered why I had avoided this task for so long.

I have asked our financial advisor, on several occasions, if there was any reason to keep all of these old records. Each time I was gently told "No," but it wasn't until today that I took action.

Why is it hard to let go of that which is clearly useless? Is it a matter of trust? Am I trying to keep a paper trail so that I can go back to days that were more fun? Does shredding the evidence make it undeniable that I have more history than future?

I did find a few treasures. I found my original birth certificate, a copy of my ordination certificate, a copy of a document signed by Grover Cleveland in 1886 granting a homestead easement for accessing the timber on our farm, and a handwritten letter to each of my parents that I never sent.

I am glad that I glanced at the papers and grasped ownership of what I was releasing. I feel as though I have traveled back down a road that is both crowded with trivia and marked with significance.

All of it is past. None of it can be relived. But I can filter the memories. I can choose forgiveness, gratitude, and grace. I can release the pain and embrace the joy.

I can follow the footsteps of Jesus where I am reminded that my sin has been shredded and my faith has been framed.

THE SILVER LINING OF A BRUTAL WINTER

I paid close attention as I heard these unexpected words from my friend, "This has been a wonderful winter." Those of you who live in southern Wisconsin will understand why I was so taken aback by this comment. I, myself, have been heard to say, "This is the first time in my entire life that relocating to a warmer climate has some appeal."

I like seasons, usually. It is just that this winter has been so brutal and unrelenting. If it is not subzero temperatures, it is snowing with treacherous drifting and wind chills that are subzero.

I listened carefully as my friend, who works with our State government, explained that these brutal conditions were solving problems that were beyond human solution. Among them were the survival of our elm trees as the borer larvae is frozen, toxic algae in our lakes being reduced, and our water levels being stabilized.

Is God taking care of His creation by doing what needs to be done for it to flourish?

Does this create a metaphor for what may be a hidden agenda for the times when I feel like I am shivering in a cold wind that has no purpose?

Maybe I need a season of perceived "brutal conditions" in order for that which needs to be cleansed from my life to be overcome.

Can I trust, today, that what seems harsh to me is an act of grace for which someday I will be grateful?

HE PUTS MY TEARS IN A BOTTLE

When I am tempted to doubt God's care for my sadness, I am reminded of Psalm 56 that tells me He keeps my tears in a bottle. They must be precious to Him.

I cherish the times in my life when I have an experience that leaves me with the thought, "That must be just a glimpse of how God feels."

Yesterday my six-year-old granddaughter was sad. I wasn't sure what her sadness was about, but I knelt beside her and said, "I know you don't have school next week. Why don't we plan to have some special time together?" In response, tears started flowing down her cheeks. She was not actively crying, just quietly shedding tears. She swallowed hard a couple of times and then said, "Maybe we could go for a doughnut."

I said, "Come here and let Besta (my Norwegian name for Grandma) hold you." As she snuggled into my arms, the thought came that even if I have to drive across the whole country to find one, we will have a doughnut together next week.

If my feeble love can respond to tears with that resolve, how can I ever doubt the love response of the one who keeps my tears in a bottle?

O TASTE AND SEE...

Having prayed through Paul's prayers in my morning devotions, I was gripped by this phrase in the Amplified Bible "(That you may really come) to know (practically, through experience for yourselves) the love of Christ, which far surpasses mere knowledge (without experience)."

I determined that I had an hour left before I needed to get ready for work. I turned off all the lights in the house, settled down with my coffee in a comfortable lounge chair with some soft "soaking" music in the background and asked God to let me experience His love personally.

It was the time of the day where night meets morning. I looked out into the darkness of our backyard, knowing that light would soon win. Then my heart leapt within me. I thought I saw something moving in the dark. Was it only shadows? Was it my imagination? No! As I looked closer, there were vague outlines of real movement.

Flooded with joy, I recognized two deer enjoying the breakfast I had prepared for them. Yesterday, trudging through the snow and cold, I had carried a pail of crushed corn and filled two aluminum basins at the back of our yard. This morning, I watched as these beautiful creatures tasted and saw that it was good.

I sensed God whisper, "Your joy is just a scratch on the surface of what I feel for you when you devour what I have prepared for you."

O taste and see…

READ THE END OF THE BOOK

I am preparing for a Memorial Service I did not expect to attend. The person who is being remembered is younger than I am. If I let my natural mind calculate, she died too early.

I also need to process the trajectory of her story. The earlier pages record a woman who loved and served Jesus, but for many years now, physical and mental pain has shadowed this earlier experience.

This is not the testimony that we are comfortable presenting. We want to be able to produce concrete examples of seeing the goodness of the Lord in the land of the living.

The story of this life leaves us with more questions than answers.

But to Whom do we take our questions?

Why do we scramble for answers?

How do we explain to her children that our faith has not wavered even though, in this story, God has planted His footprints in the sea and rode upon the storm?

How do we acknowledge that our behaviors have consequences without picking up a stone?

Does God need to be defended or is He asking to be trusted?

I remember a day when the husband of the woman for whom this service is being held was a leader in preschool ministry with me. This memory is vivid.

We were a group of children's ministry leaders analyzing the need for preschool Sunday School teachers and realized we were tragically short. The mood of the group was somber until this leader stood up and with two words reoriented us all:

"Read the end of the book: JESUS WINS!!!!"

GRATEFUL FOR HERITAGE

My grandmother was baptized
in this church in 1876. It is
still standing, wrapped by the
mountains and waterfalls of
Telemark, Norway.

It was my privilege to kneel at
this altar and pray, "Fader vår,
du som er i himmelen,

helliget vorde ditt navn"; the words of the Lord's Prayer she
had taught me when I was first learning to speak.

My grandmother crossed the ocean in 1892 at the age of
16. Famine in this land of stunning beauty forced her father
to make the agonizing decision to send her to America.
She worked for her uncle in this strange land, walking
behind a plow for two years, making just fifty cents a week.

I crossed this same ocean to find my grandmother's home
in the comfort of a relatively short flight. I have been able
to visit her country on many occasions, always
remembering the first time I stepped off the plane and
found myself standing on Norwegian soil. Tears ran down

my cheeks with the overwhelming sense that I was home.

I am grateful for my heritage and for the blessing of being able to trace my roots. My family history reminds me that I have been rescued from poverty into affluence. I am the beneficiary of prayers prayed and a price paid.

As awesome as this story is to me, it pales in remembrance of what Papa God has done, sending His Son to Calvary for me. Now I am a joint heir with Him Who intercedes for me.

Thank you, Father, for my heritage.

*F*OOTSTEPS IN THE SEA

Faith Through Aging Eyes encounters God when He plants His footsteps in the sea.

We have precious memories of being able to track the God we love and trust. We are eager to tell of the times when His interventions in our life are so profound that we are invited to share them from the platform.

But none of us are strangers to the stories that don't tell themselves so easily. The times when, even though we refuse to let our faith crack, doubt pounds relentlessly.

The God we have learned to track in soft wet sand now plants His footprints in the sea. Often we can still track Him in many areas of our life, but there is one that simply won't identify itself as a picture of God's care.

If we dare to name it, we would say we feel abandoned.

We know how to preach to ourselves. We know how to claim promises. We are tempted to hide our pain because we don't want to be a discouragement to those whose lives are overflowing with praise.

Maybe we learn something from Jesus' journey to Gethsemane.

He told most of his disciples to wait while He separated Himself from them.

He brought three trusted friends with Him and poured out His heart to them.

He then went alone to the Father and there encountered the One Who gave Him the power to walk to the cross.

WATCH FOR THE YELLOW ARROW

It's been more than six months since I walked the Camino de Santiago in northern Spain. The path is quite unpredictable, even with the help of guidebooks that tell you what to expect. The distance is longer, the hills are steeper, and the terrain is an invitation to stumble.

Everything in you wants to ask, "Are we almost there?" but you don't ask because you are afraid of the answer. If it weren't for the yellow arrow, I don't know if I would have mustered the courage to endure.

Everyone knows the yellow arrow marks the path, assuring you that you are not lost and your destination lies ahead.

Sometimes the yellow arrow is obvious.

Other times, the distance between the arrows is concerning.

But finally one appears. You may need to look closely, but it's there.

59

It hardly needs to be stated; the similarity of this metaphor to life.

I only want to encourage you to watch for the yellow arrow. It may come through a friend, a dream, a scripture, an experience, hearing someone else's story. But the arrow will be there.

Thus says the Lord, "Stand in the ways and see, and ask for the old paths, where the good way is, and walk in it, then you will find rest for your souls..." (Jeremiah 6:16 NKJV)

AFTER FORTY YEARS

One morning I made a video Skype call to a friend I'd met 40 years earlier at an international Bible School held on an island off the south coast of Norway. She was from Scotland and I was from the United States, although I took every opportunity given to share that my grandmother was born in Telemark, Norway. In my mind I had come home to this place.

I wondered, as I dialed my friend, if it would be like talking to a stranger. Have I changed? Has she changed? Would we remember the same things? Would we find anything to talk about?

The experience at the Bible School had been intense regarding our experiences of God from a global perspective and experiences of knowing believers from other parts of the world. This friend and I had become especially close.

We wrote back and forth over the years on the blue airmail paper that was the primary way of contact back then. With the onset of the computer, we exchanged a few emails. But today we would see each other's faces and hear each other's voices again. After a few moments of sharing the unimportant things with each other, all small talk was over. Once again we shared only that which was deeply important to us. We shared with trust and with the familiarity of a proven friendship.

If you have had a close relationship that time has interrupted, I encourage you to make contact. It is a joy to know that we can pick up where we left off. It may be at an even more significant place than where we left off as God has had 40 years to do transformational work.

AND CLOSE THE PATH OF MISERY

Sometimes when I have trouble praying, I go to my old hymnbook and look for something that will give me a jump-start. This morning I was impacted by these words from an advent hymn dated 1710. The first lines are "O come, O come Emmanuel," but the stanza that grabbed my attention was in the last verse: "Make safe the way that leads on high and close the path to misery."

I am sure a case can be made for the author to have been referring to the redemption that becomes available through the coming of Our Lord Jesus Christ.

But today, these words spoke to me on a smaller scale. I have recognized that there is a thought pattern path in my life that leads to misery. When I allow the enemy to deliver fear along this path my joy vanishes.

My prayer today is that the Holy Spirit closes this path for me. I seem helpless to do it on my own. I am asking God to put up a detour sign on the path that leads to misery and direct me, instead, to the way that leads on high.

A MEDAL AND MEMORIES

The Wisconsin Senior Olympic event that was scheduled at the zoo had to be canceled because of heat and humidity. My head knew this was a wise call but my heart sank. I wanted to do this power walk. "Well," I said with resignation, "I can wait until next year."

Not much later I received a call asking if I could participate in a rescheduled event at the lakefront. Of course I not only could but I would. And I did!!!

The friend who introduced me to this adventure is a 5K runner. She walked with me. I was aware that her capacity far exceeds mine but she didn't focus on that. If her goal was to make it fun for me, then she absolutely won this event.

Because it had been rescheduled, it lacked some of the ceremony one would expect, but we had a clear starting point, a starting signal, a prescribed route, a stopwatch, and a finishing point. Our time for a five-kilometer power walk was forty-three minutes and fifty-two seconds. This time was officially recorded and I was challenged to beat that record the next year. I was given a t-shirt and a ribbon with a Wisconsin Olympic Medal dangling off the end.

It's hard to describe why this activity brought so much excitement. Was it because I was chasing away some of the myths about aging and decreased mobility? Was it because doing this lets the kid in me come out and play? I don't know but I can't wait to sign up again next year.

I cherish the memories from that walk as God used them to remind me that He is walking the path of my life with me. Let your imagination help you frame this picture.

We had rounded a corner on the track and were walking through an area with a beautiful lagoon on the right and Lake Drive on the left. I looked the part with my headphones blaring fast-stepping music, water bottle in my waist pack, and stopwatch around my neck. My whole focus was to finish this race and finish it fast. I was moving my feet, making sure my whole foot rolled onto the ground, and arms were pumping in rhythm. My breathing started to concern me but I knew I needed to ignore it.

Suddenly I felt hands on my shoulders. Their touch was so gentle that I didn't startle or lose my stride. Then with firmness they guided me to the right side of the path. Before I knew why I was directed this way, a biker whizzed right by us. Safe again, the hands were released from my shoulders. We walked on without comment. I am comforted now by remembering the gentleness and strength of those hands. I am glad my friend walked with me.

As we were nearing the finish line, I began to relax and was planning on coasting in. "Come on, now," my friend coached, "let's put a little more energy into this. The finish line is in sight." Finding strength from somewhere, I pushed harder. When we stepped over the finish line, I felt I had finished well.

I have a medal hanging on a hook with my t-shirt right beside it. Both will fade with time, but I will always have the memories of my friend who demonstrated in the natural world the way I walk with Jesus. This walk will grow only brighter with time.

CELEBRATING THE SILVER LINING

I made a phone call this week to a couple from our church fellowship. They are both 89 years old. The wife answered and said her husband, who is a retired physician, was at the hospital praying with patients. She said that his legs were bad so after he walks the equivalent of four blocks that he would need to come home.

I mentioned I hadn't seen them for a while and wanted to check in. She said they had so much to be thankful for but didn't make it to church very often. I asked if I could renew their membership for them. She said, "Oh, yes, it is still our church. When we can't get there, we send our tithe in the mail."

I asked if there was anything they needed. She responded that a couple from our church lived across the street and were very attentive. She did confess that she didn't clean the way she did in the past but laughingly added that it didn't really matter because neither one of them see very well.

I reflected on the richness of this conversation, thanking God for the testimony of their story, hoping that this would be representative of my story, and eventually conceded that I already look better in dim light.

*D*RIVEN BY GRATITUDE

I was walking out of the chapel recently having just led a Memorial Service for one of our seniors when I met her. She seemed to be searching for something or someone so I asked if I could help. She was clearly from another country, an Asian country, but was articulate with English. She answered my question by asking if she could go into the chapel and pray.

I said yes, but there were mourners in there and a youth group would be filling it soon. I asked if I could help her find a place that would be quiet. She expressed deep appreciation at the offer. I then introduced myself as a pastor and asked if she wanted someone to pray with her or if she preferred to pray alone.

She said if someone would pray with her that would be even better. I escorted her to our prayer room. As we walked there, I asked if she knew Jesus. She said, "Yes," explaining that her mother had converted to Christianity.

When we settled into the prayer room, I asked her what she would specifically like to talk to God about. She said she just wanted to say "Thank You." She explained that God had given her so much.

I prayed and then she prayed. She simply thanked God for everything He had done for her and given to her.

I wonder why so few people come into a church or prayer room just to say thank you. When Jesus asked, "Where are the nine?" He was referring to the ten lepers He had just healed. All ten walked away having experienced this amazing healing, but only one came back to say "Thank you."

Am I one of the nine?

I WONDER IF I BROUGHT SALT

I am driving in my car hoping I have everything I need to spend a few days at our camper. It takes one hour and fifteen minutes to get from my back door to the camper's front door. How and why we have this camper on this lakefront rental site is a story too long to tell here. It is enough to review my annual mental conflict.

I should sell this thing. It's more work than it's worth. The rent is expensive and every year is laden with repair bills. I spend most of my time setting up and cleaning up. By the time I get it together, I don't have the time or energy to enjoy it.

But I get there and a heron is fishing just a few feet from our deck. Something of my childhood stirs within me as I check the stack of firewood. The sparks from the campfire tonight will shoot high and as I follow the spark, I will see a star. God's creation presses me to worship. Besides, in this economy no one will buy it for a fair price.

Let's get back to the salt. Why can't I remember if I left some there, or if I brought some with me? Am I getting forgetful, or have I always been this disorganized? I can argue both views with the persuasion of a Yale attorney.

As I engage in this internal debate, I find my thoughts wandering to my final journey when I leave this body known as a tent and move into my eternal home. I smile as I remember that I won't need to remember to bring anything.

Because of the scars on Jesus' hands, I can come home with empty hands.

My Dad's favorite hymn fills my mind and heart.

> *Rock of Ages, cleft for me,*
> *let me hide myself in Thee…*
> *Nothing in my hands I bring,*
> *simply to Thy cross I cling.* *

What does arriving at heaven's door empty-handed mean to you?

Rock of Ages, Cleft for Me,
  Text: Augustus M. Toplady, Music: Thomas Hastings

DON'T ASK ME AGAIN!!!

My mother kept asking the same questions. It took me a couple of years to really face the fact that she asked again and again because she had no memory of having asked before. As her dementia progressed, there were episodes where the questions came in a rapid-fire cycle of repetition.

She asked, "Where's Daddy?" I said, "Daddy died." She gasped and asked, "When?" I said, "Ten years ago." She asked, "What did he die from?" I said, "His heart gave out."

With no space in between, the conversation repeated:

She asked, "Where's Daddy?" I said, "Daddy died." She gasped and asked, "When?" I said "Ten years ago." She asked, "What did he die from?" I said, "His heart gave out."

With no space in between, the conversation repeated:

She asked, "Where's Daddy?" I said, "Daddy died." She gasped and asked, "When?" I said, "Ten years ago." She asked, "What did he die from?" I said, "His heart gave out."

I then told myself I couldn't keep saying the same thing over and over and gave myself permission to try a verbal stun gun.

On this round when she asked, "Where's Daddy?" I said, "Daddy died." She gasped and asked, "When?" I said, "Ten years ago." She asked, "What did he die from?" I said, "He died from too much sex!" "Oh," Mom said with a shudder and a smile, "THEN I KILLED HIM!"

She had no more questions!

And neither did I!!!

I DID ALL I COULD

I stood beside my dad. We were leaning together on the fence that formed a boundary for our pigs, watching the mother pig nurse her new litter. The mother pig had gradually grown to look like a big balloon. There were many places on her tummy where her newborn babies could connect their mouth for their first taste of milk.

Their bed was plain dirt at best, and mud at worst, but they all seemed happy. Well, almost all. As we watched, the mother repeatedly nudged the smallest baby away from her tummy. I asked my dad why the mother would push the smallest one away. Dad simply said, "Because she knows that one is going to die." I asked Dad if I could have that one. Dad said, "Yes, you can have it, but you need to know it is going to die."

I ran for a shoebox and padded it with a blanket. I found a little bottle with a nipple and filled it with milk. The baby pig drank. I set my alarm for every two hours during the night. During the day I had a job of picking cucumbers. I carefully positioned the baby pig in the shoebox and took it with me to work, leaving the pig in the sunshine at the end of my row. I picked faster than anyone so I would have time to feed the baby and still keep up with the crew.

After several days of giving my best, the little pig died. I guess I had to learn what the mother pig already knew.

I'm glad I had a dad who didn't protect me from the realities of life. He let me experience pain and loss. He let me try.

The end of the story is not what I had hoped, but the memory speaks to the riches of my childhood and the wisdom of my parents.

What would you answer if a child were to ask you the questions I asked my dad?

I CAN'T FIND MY GLASSES

Two friends and I spent time talking around a small table. A few minutes after we all went our separate ways, one friend came back to the place we had met and asked if I had seen her glasses. Together we looked but to no avail.

After searching everywhere, this friend called the third friend and asked if she might possibly have picked up the missing glasses.

Follow this conversation:

Could you possibly have picked up my glasses?

Do they have brown frames?

Yes.

I think I have them. I think I am wearing them!!

Can you see out of them?

No!

What are you doing?

The laundry.

Well, I will have to come and get them because I can't see without them!!

End of conversation.

It is high risk to have old friends, but very precious and lots of material for laughter.

RESTING WITH JESUS

I asked her if she would pray with me before she went back to India.

She is my friend's mother and has been a missionary in her native India for decades. Every summer she spends time here with her daughter, son-in-law, and grandchildren. This gives me a chance to see God through the eyes of someone from another culture who has grown to know and love Him.

I am always surprised when I hug her to once again realize how short she is. I don't think of her as little because there is such power in her presence, in her speech, and in her prayers.

I arrived at her daughter's home for this requested time of prayer. As the three of us settled into seats in the living room, the mother picked up her chair and moved it towards mine. "I want to be closer to you," she said.

Somehow our conversation drifted toward waking up in the morning in the presence of Jesus. I listened attentively to this perspective.

Just BE with Jesus when you wake up. You can talk to Him or you can just BE still. Just REST on His lap the way a child falls asleep on her father's lap. If you are reading and you fall asleep, that is okay.

After you have had this time of BEING with Jesus, you will start the day refreshed. Then you don't need to worry about what you are supposed to DO. He will have everything under His control. You can just ENJOY THE SHOW.

She prayed for me, talking intimately with expectancy to the God Who has sustained her as a widow, is giving her strength to serve Him with vigor, and reveals Himself through her faith.

A few days after she left for India, I asked her daughter about her trip home. "Oh," she said, "Mom is covered with a kind of travel grace. Something always happens. This time she was seated in a row with two men. The stewardess came and asked the men if she could move them to other seats. After the men moved, pillows and blankets were brought and Mom stretched out and slept the whole trip."

I wonder if this lady told her friends that God had been gracious in His provision of rest or had this provision become a natural expectation?

More than a year later I was deeply blessed to be standing at her bedside in a hospital. She was laughing and talking with the medical staff when she simply folded her body to the left and breathed her last breath on earth.

I can only imagine her waking up on Jesus' lap and finishing her sentence.

May I learn to rest in Jesus' lap with such intimacy that leaving this tent is simply the next step of the journey.

I'M STILL YOUNG... I THINK

I want to commend you for your courage in reading this book, especially since your secret is that you feel like you are just getting started. Do you remember the first time someone gave you the impression that you were an older person? Has anyone ever said or done anything to indicate to you that, in his or her eyes, you were moving right along with the aging process?

A couple of weeks ago, the person who coordinates the prison ministry at our church told me she needed an elderly Christian for a one-time visit to an inmate. At first I thought she wanted me to find her someone, and then it slowly dawned on me that she wanted me. It took my mind a few moments to adjust to that thought.

Sometimes the message is mixed. A few years ago I took a trip to Mali, Africa. In preparation, I needed a number of vaccinations. When the travel clinic nurse realized I did not have immunity to measles, she said that because of my age I would have to get special permission from my doctor. I felt offended but went ahead and got the permission she wanted. When I finally went in for the shots, I was asked to sign a waiver stating I would not get pregnant for 28 days!!!!!

Aging is not an easy topic in our culture. Just looking at birthday cards tells us that people don't know what to say. I am quite amazed at the many things our advertisers say we can buy to interrupt or even reverse signs of aging…and yet time is rather relentless in its pursuit.

What have you experienced that lets you know that others see you as getting older even though older to you means "they" and not "we?"

WHEN DO I SAY GOODBYE?

I have said *goodbye* to two precious friends this year because I knew they were dying. One was hospitalized for kidney failure after learning that the chemotherapy she had been enduring for her cancer was no longer effective. As a Christian, a medical doctor, and a psychologist, she applied what she knew to be true about having exhausted every human effort.

The day before this friend died, she was given the gift of vitality, which allowed her to bless her family and her close friends. My *goodbye* was not done in person. When I asked if she wanted me to come, she said firmly, "Roselyn, no. We will do this by phone." (She was in a hospital three hours away.) We both knew this was the last time we would talk on this earth. Our *goodbye* was painful but it brought closure to this journey of friendship.

The other was a retired teacher who became a hobby farmer. Having been made Power of Attorney for his healthcare and finances, I was sorry I lived two hours away from the hospital he was in. We had been friends since childhood and were pretty much able to finish each other's sentences. His farm was often a refuge for me from the rush of suburban life. I knew his health was failing, but I didn't expect the call I received from the ICU nurse who told me his heart rhythm was incompatible with life.

I told her to tell him I loved him and I would see him in heaven. She answered, "Oh, honey, his heart just stopped." Again, it was a painful *goodbye* but one I can remember as the end of our walking together in this life.

I have other friends where the time to say *goodbye* is not so easily defined. How do you process the loss when the enemy is dementia, mental illness, or a stroke? How do you handle the occasional breakthroughs when things seem to be as they used to be for a brief time? I don't know much about heaven, but I look forward to eternity where we will never have to be separated and never say *goodbye*.

*T*HE POWER OF LOVE

I would say that I am a careful driver. I am attentive to road conditions and aware of traffic patterns. Red lights prompt me to stop and green lights send me on my way. I will yield, merge, and right turn only when a sign so instructs and will not right turn when a sign prohibits.

The exception to this diligent obedience is adhering to speed limits. If 40 MPH seems safe to me, I don't see why I should crawl along at 25 MPH if there is no school zone and no rationale for the decision. In fact, I find myself impatient with the occasional driver that gets in my way by taking these speed limit signs seriously.

But today I have a new perspective. Today I drove the speed limit. I watched for the sign, lined my speedometer to it, and clicked the cruise control. Cars pulled up behind me, realized I was ignoring their attempts to get me moving faster, and whipped around me.

Why did I change? It's not because I was given a ticket. It's not because I have had an accident. It's not because I read a book or listened to a lecture. The change is simply a response to being loved.

A couple of days ago my "adopted" son rode with me as I ran an errand that required more than two hours of driving. He was quiet for almost a half hour and then commented that I had a lead foot. I agreed in a way that seemed I was almost proud of it. Before long he reminded me again of what the speed limit was and what my speed was registering. He made sure I noticed a half-hidden police car.

It slowly sunk in that this younger man was concerned about my driving fast because he cared about me. As I processed his remarks, I found them grounded in wisdom, some of which he has learned the hard way.

In the few years that I have known him, we have developed a bond that can best be described as mother and son. During this time, we have navigated some bumps in the road. Sometimes my visits to him have been in the county jail. Sometimes I have listened as a counselor, confronted as a parent, or encouraged as a pastor.

We are now in a new season where *mother and son* is the best descriptor of our relationship. Today he is the teacher and I am the learner. I am driving the speed limit today not because I think it is a good idea or even necessary; I am obeying because it is important to someone who loves me.

I wonder how often we rationalize God's laws, placing them under the authority of their making sense to us.

Would it be easier to live in obedience if we did so simply because the One who wrote the laws loves us? How do you decide when to be obedient and why?

*S*TILL MISSING MY DAD

My dad died 15 years ago. I was given the gift of standing beside his hospital bed in our den when he breathed his final breath.

His death was not a surprise, but it was a shock. We had been prepared, but there is no way to truly be prepared for the loss of someone you so deeply love. The gratitude I felt for his being released from the body that had stopped working competed with the pain of the little girl in me that desperately needed her daddy. I was 53 years old.

I am thinking a lot about him today because today is his birthday.

Grief is a lonely thing in that nobody really gets what it is you are missing. There are some things that only the person who is now gone would really understand. I don't even know what to call what I am feeling today or if I need to give it a name at all. Dad and I didn't use words very often when we were together, so it seems odd to try to describe our relationship with words.

There was the day when the wind and the rain leveled a field of golden oats ready for harvest. I saw dad standing on our back porch watching the storm rob us of essential income. I did the only thing I could do. I walked out on the porch and stood by his side. Neither of us talked. I stood with him until he was ready to come in the house and then we walked in together. I think I was about 10 years old. He was my dad, but in that moment we were friends.

In the spring he would plow a field all the way from our county road to the start of our pine woods. The first furrow had to be straight as an arrow. He would set his eyes on a goal and guide that sputtering John Deere tractor through the unmarked ground with never a crook or a curve. When we drove down that county road, we would both look at the straight furrow and smile. He was proud of it, and I was proud of him.

Sometimes Dad made Mom nervous. I tried to assure her that he could handle all the different situations, but she didn't always share my confidence. One of those times was during hunting season when many hunters used our driveway to make their way back into the woods to hunt deer. The game warden would usually come and park outside our granary and check to make sure the hunters had bought a tag.

As Mom watched out the window, she knew that the granary door was blocking the warden's view of the deer Dad had shot, for which he didn't have a tag. Dad just stood there and told jokes to the game warden. When the game warden left, Dad came in and he and I would laugh as Mom scolded and reminded us of the fine we could have received.

Last year during an ice storm I was on a road that was taking me up a high hill. I was about to turn around when I remembered that Dad would have made it up that hill. I put the car in the lowest gear and began the icy crawl to the top. When I came over the crest, I smiled. My dad may have died 15 years ago but there is a lot of him left in me.

What memories are shaping your life today?

I LOVED YOU RIGHT AWAY

I received an email from a precious friend asking me to rejoice with her about the birth of her first grandchild. It prompted the memory of this poem that I wrote almost five years ago after I had appointed myself to be the adopted grandmother for the coming baby of my Australian co-worker.

Since this child already had a grandmother in the area and another in Australia, I used the name Besta, which is "grandmother" in Norwegian. I held her in the hospital just a few hours after her birth.

This poem captures the stunning beauty of the gift of our first encounter.

> *I Loved You Right Away*
>
> *I thought I'd grow to love you*
>
> *When I learned how you'd been knit.*
>
> *I thought I'd need to know you*
>
> *And how you and I would fit.*
>
> *I thought I'd need to see you smile*

And maybe dry your tears,

To learn how I could make you laugh

And take away your fears.

I thought we'd play together

And maybe read a book,

We'd watch the fish and catch a frog

And maybe learn to cook.

Love, I thought, would be a seed

That I would guard and shower

Until one day it sprouted forth

A bud, and then a flower.

But, love for you had other plans

There's nothing I can say

'cept when my eyes first saw you

I loved you right away.

PS: And so I'll say I love you

And not try to explain

For God has opened heaven's gates

With unexpected rain.

Some day you'll call me Besta

Then we'll ponder, you and I

And together thank Our Father

Who won't need to ask us why!

From Besta Roselyn 10/06/06

She calls me Besta now. I took a picture of her with my cat and I asked how the two of them were the same. She said, "We are both yours." I rested in the arms of joy.

I want to give this joy to Papa God. I want to tell Him often that I am resting in the joy of knowing I am His.

Faith Through Aging Eyes opens opportunities to ask God, "Who would I be if I wasn't a wife, a pastor, a teacher...?"

His answer that never changes is, "MINE!"

THE PIECE DOESN'T FIT

As a child, once in a while I would buy a puzzle from the dime store. It would have a picture on the front and when the pieces were turned right side up, you could tell that they belonged somewhere in that puzzle because of their shading and shape. It was very unsettling to get most of the puzzle together and realize that there were a couple of pieces that fit nowhere. Did they wind up in the wrong box?

This is the feeling I had the day I heard about a tragic outbreak of violence in Norway. It is the country of my heritage. The emigrant community I grew up in did not have locks for our doors. This is the country I visit where I can rest, trust, watch entire families walk together in the parks on Sunday, and hear stories of how the king shops for groceries with everyone else.

I have nowhere to put this piece of news that a youth camp was invaded and that place of refuge is now referred to as hell. This same dilemma presents when I try to put the pieces of my life experience into the framework of what I perceive to be Christian pilgrimage or biblical Christianity.

I read promises of how God will respond when we are faithful. Most of the time the pieces fit, but there is often one or two that seem to have come from a different box.

These feelings come to me through witnessing the suffering of a friend or the dashed hopes of someone I love. I can't throw out the whole puzzle but I can't throw away the pieces either. I need to decide if my faith is based on what I can see or on the One Who sees what I can't.

Do the pieces not fit because I don't see the bigger picture? Is my frame too small? God grant me the grace to trust you when life doesn't fit easily into place. May I yield that which I cannot explain because I know the signature on the puzzle is Love.

I WANT TO BE LIKE HIM

I watched two men working together today.

The older man is a weaving of creativity, ingenuity, perseverance, and skill. He has driven on some rough roads, hit some potholes, woken up in a ditch, scratched a path to greener pastures, and recognized the joy of investing in an eager learner.

The younger man watches his mentor's every move. He listens to instruction. He humbly dismisses praise. He is quick to laugh because the relationship is safe. He is quick to say "Thank you." He is very aware of being invested in.

When I asked the younger man to tell me about his life dreams, he looked at the older man and said, "I want to be like him." They both smiled.

I get to watch them again tomorrow. I want to learn from each of them. I want for someone to someday want to be like me because I chose to invest in him or her. I want to be intentional in my gratitude to Jesus for making it possible for me to become like Him. He is molding me into His image. It's too amazing to describe, but I get to wait and watch as He works.

We will be like Him when we see Him as He is.

Ask me about my dream. I will tell you I want to be like Him.

MY FIRST PAIR OF SKIS

They were a Christmas present. Dad had ripped two boards about four feet long and four inches wide. The board was crafted into a gradual point on one end. The point itself was about a one-inch square. All of this I learned only after receiving them at Christmas because they were carefully hidden from me.

For many weeks, after I had gone to bed, Dad would put the pointed end of these boards into the reservoir of our wood stove. He would remove them in the morning, gradually shaping the warped end so that the board curled. These boards were painted red on the top. The bottom was coated with the kind of wax Mom used to top off her canning of strawberry jam. I could keep a piece of this wax to refresh the coat if it wore down.

These "skis" were fastened to my feet by two leather straps that had been riveted to each side of the ski. They were just the length that allowed my rubber overshoes to fit snugly.

I could hardly wait to get back to school after Christmas vacation. Some of the bigger boys from our one-room school had built a ski jump on a high hill just across the road. At recess we all carried our skies and stomped over to the hill. When my turn came, I skied down the slope quick as lightening and jumped high in the air, landing on my feet.

I looked pretty good, I think, but I knew it was not personal skill. It was all because of my equipment.

One of the benefits of *Faith Through Aging Eyes* is being able to reflect on our story and recognize that experiences that once seemed random are now necessary for the challenges of today.

I am grateful that the God who knit me together in my mother's womb continues to weave my story.

I am glad that no color is wasted as the Artist creates His Masterpiece!

IRREFUTABLE INDICANTS OF AGING

I find myself most at home with those who may look old to other people but don't feel old themselves. I find it amusing that people more than 80 years old don't want to join a senior group because they don't want to be around old people. I find it amusing, but I do understand. I am shocked when my own denial of aging is brought into the light of reality.

Life is kind in regularly providing us with irrefutable indicants.

I received an invitation this week for a high school class reunion. All classes that had graduated 50 years ago or more are invited. The event starts at 10 a.m. rather than the 4 p.m. I have come to expect. The party finishes at 4 p.m. rather than extending into the early morning hours. Is it possible that this is a gathering of old people? If so, why am I invited?

I went for a walk today. It was a beautiful day but just a little windy. I wore knit jogging pants and a sweatshirt. I also brought a headband to protect my ears. I met many walkers and runners on the path. Most had shorts and tank tops. None had a head covering. Why am I wearing so many clothes? Do those who meet me think they have met an old person?

I am finding myself delighted when a younger person struggles to remember something. If someone who is obviously young gets a date confused or is unable to come up with a name, I feel like celebrating inside. Is it because I don't want my memory loss to be related to aging?

What irrefutable indicants of aging have you encountered?

*L*EAVING FOOTPRINTS

I visited a new baby in his home. The baby was five days old. His parents looked on him with a sense of reverence as they took delight in his few minutes of being wide awake. It was a joy for me to hold him and share in the wonder of this new life.

Before I left, we leaned over the baby, who was cuddled in his father's arms, and thanked God for knitting him together in his mother's womb and making him physically perfect. We prayed that he would become an image-bearer of Jesus. It was good to be embraced by the miracle of birth.

I then picked up my husband and drove to the home of a ninety-one-year-old man who is now on hospice home care. I have known him for several years; he and his wife have been pillars in our Senior Adult Ministry.

He was propped in a large chair, wearing pajamas and a robe. He, just like the baby described above, needed to be carried from his bed that very morning. After a gracious greeting, he told me he had been praying all weekend to go home and be with Jesus. He looked deep into my eyes and asked, "What possible use can I be now?"

I asked him to reflect on his life and give me three things that he would want a five-day-old baby to know.

He took a deep breath and said, one, believe that the Lord Jesus died for your sins, two, God is always in control, and three, ask and you will receive.

I thanked him for these wise comments and promised to pass them along to the parents of the baby.

Remembering this old man needed meaning and purpose, I told him he could be praying for this baby.

The old man said, "Let's do that right now."

The prayer went something like this: "Thank you, Lord, for the gift you have given to these parents by the loving arms of Jesus. May your rich blessing be upon this child and may he grow to know Jesus as his Lord and Savior."

I believe the life of this baby will be different because of the prayers of this dying man. I am not usually one to focus on numbers, but I calculated that the old man had lived 33,239 days. The baby had only been alive for five days.

Not many days later it was my privilege to lead the Memorial Service for this man. During my message I invited the parents and this baby to come up and we thanked God that he had prayed for this child.

What are you doing today that will make your Memorial Service full of footprints that lead to Jesus?

WHEN DID WE SEE YOU HUNGRY?

The picture that Jesus uses in Matthew 25 where He says that when you feed the hungry you are actually feeding Him has always been impactful to me. I have often taken refuge in the phrase "whatever you did for one of these." That measurement makes the task more doable. I can feed one, clothe one, or visit one sick person, yet I don't find the little I do very comforting when I look around my home and see that I have accumulated more than I need to live well.

The challenge has increased now that I am working with a benevolence ministry where we are stewarding contributions that people are "giving to God's work" and distributing these funds to those who come hungry. I believe that some of those who come are those that Jesus will reference when He says to me, "I was hungry, and you fed me." It is also true that some who come asking for practical help would actually be better off if we confront poor choices.

God has sent us a highly qualified team for this work. I can refer to this team and know that each story will be listened to and trusted discernment will guide us. But, there is a danger here that we don't start to depend on ourselves. We need to listen to each story on our knees and borrow the words of the Old Testament king who said we don't know what to do but our eyes are on You.

The decisions we make will matter for eternity. God, help us to recognize when You are hungry. Thank you for honoring the hungry, naked stranger and the sick so highly that you borrow their identity.

When have you seen Jesus hungry this week?

A SIMPLE PLAN

In John's gospel, Jesus talks to Peter about what will happen when Peter gets old. We can read these verses in John 21 and learn about God's plan for Peter. We can read these verses and be glad that it is improbable that we will be crucified upside down so that God can be glorified. But, we can also look for that which might apply to our lives today and seek God's heart for what is important to Him.

I have found four steps that I want to practice in the days, weeks, and years ahead. Maybe you will try them too.

Tell Jesus I Love Him

I can do this with words. I can sing Him a song. I can read Him a Psalm. I can write Him a Psalm…

Feed His Sheep

I can visit my friend who is sick. I can pray prayers that "make God sweat." I can do an act of service for someone. I can pay another's bill without telling them. I can share my testimony with all who need to hear…

Die to Anything He Can Use to Glorify Himself

I can let my losses happen. I can grieve but not as those who have no hope. I can ask for and then embrace the grace to be diminished…

Follow Him

I can sit in His Presence each day and let Him direct my steps. I can take risks by saying "Yes" to things that terrify me, because He has a way of doing through me what I could never do on my own. I can care for His creation. I can say "Yes" before I hear the request…

What have you learned from God's perspective on getting older? Have you found a simple plan?

*F*INGERPRINTS OF HOPE

I have heard a report of a residential home for cognitively challenged children where they have completely given up trying to keep a picture window free of fingerprints. The children, if not interrupted for activities of daily living, would spend hours each day with their fingers and noses pressed against the glass window. The reason they give is one that is so obvious to them that they wonder why anyone would ask. They say they are watching for Jesus to come back.

In what position will He find my hands when He returns?

Will they be wrung in despair?

Will they be folded in prayer?

Will they be blistered from service?

Will they be pressed, with expectation of His coming, against whatever glass is hemming me in?

TAKE MY HAND

I was walking through the lobby of our church at the time when our preschool children use this place as a kind of playground. I heard the patter of many little feet before I saw them running at full speed along a prescribed path. They were about three years old. I watched as a little boy near the end of the line stumbled and fell. He got up on his own and as he did the expression of his face was ambivalent. He was clearly trying to decide if he should cry.

Before he had time to decide, the little boy next in line took his hand and gave him a big smile. The boy who fell caught the smile and beamed back. Hand in hand they continued running their course.

A little while later, I was looking out of the second-story window of our classroom building and saw a large sedan pull up. The lady driving was struggling to get a walker out of the trunk. When she finally did, she opened the passenger door and worked on placing the walker into a position where her friend could reach it. It took awhile to get the walker steady, remove the seatbelt, and start the process of getting this person out of the car. After several attempts, the driver placed the walker a little further from the car and extended her hand.

Her hand gave confidence and stability. After two steps hand in hand, the disabled lady grasped the walker and started the slow shuffling journey to the church door.

Watch me today, and when I stumble, take my hand.

*D*ESIGNED FOR DEPENDENCE

A common expression older people use in conversation is "I want to live as long as I can, be as independent as possible, and never be a burden." One of our most respected Christian writers has caused me to think more deeply about this subject.

John Stott, in his last book entitled *A Radical Disciple*, has chosen dependence as a

component of discipleship that is modeled by Our Lord Jesus Christ. Stott says, "You are designed to be a burden to me, and I am designed to be a burden to you."

I have often said to people who resist help, "You are not designed to make it on

your own," attempting to promote the concept of community. To take dependence to

a place of dignity is a deeper challenge. Stott reminds us that Jesus was born a dependent baby and died on a cross, unable to move, yet He was never without His dignity. Stott then concludes that if dependence was appropriate for God in the person of Jesus, it is certainly appropriate for us.

I wonder how embracing this view would affect our fear of becoming dependent or of

becoming the caretaker of someone who is dependent. Could we stop lamenting, interrupt our repetitive apologies, and risk thinking the burden we bring may actually be a blessing? The idea is like a fish swimming upstream, but it has a captivating ring of truth that makes me want to risk looking for it in my responses to people today.

What have you learned about dependence? How can we give dignity to a dependent person? How can we grant dignity to our dependent selves?

*L*INKS THAT ANCHOR TO HUMANITY

I listened with awe as Suu Kyi addressed the dignitaries who awarded her the Nobel Prize for peace. She was chosen for this honor in 1991 but because she was under house arrest in Myanmar could not personally accept it until this year.

She tried, in her address, to explain how she felt about the prize and what it meant to her. She said she hadn't really felt anything when she initially heard over the radio that she had been chosen. She went on to explain that this was because in her isolation she no longer felt a part of a bigger world.

This Nobel award drew her into the world of other humans and restored a sense of reality for her. She said that during these twenty plus years of house arrest, she had lost the links that anchor her to humanity. In reflection, however, this global recognition opened up a door in her heart.

As I listened to this amazing woman, my heart bled for the pain of my best friend who is in a prison of depression. All of the losses described by Suu are also being experienced by my friend.

I wish there was a way to open the door of my friend's heart, to tell the world that she is worthy of recognition and respect, and thereby restore the links that would anchor her to humanity.

Jesus is the lynchpin for this to happen for all of us, but we need to be able to embrace a sense of self in order to experientially benefit from a relationship with Him and with others. Our prison can be a political house arrest or a chemical depression. Both things fracture the links that anchor us to humanity.

I am so grateful that our experience of abandonment does not define the security we have as children of God.

I have beaten a familiar path to Psalm 73:21-24 (NIV).

When my heart was grieved and my spirit embittered, I was senseless and ignorant; I was a brute beast before you. Yet I am always with you; you hold me by my right hand. You guide me with your counsel, and afterward you will take me into glory.

May I never reduce the eternal promises of God to the default of my present-day struggle. I declare Glory now for all those who will shout it some day.

O FEAR OF BAD NEWS

"They will have no fear of bad news; their hearts are steadfast, trusting in the Lord."

(Psalm 112:7 NIV)

This verse is one more reminder to me that God's grace reaches far to embrace me. This is especially relevant today because I have lived in dread of bad news. Yes, of course I have reminded myself that what concerns me is in God's hands. All He does or doesn't do is driven by love. I even leaned into the old hymn that insists on the Holiness of God even though the eye of sinful man His Glory may not see.

"Holy, holy, holy, though the darkness hide thee,

Though the eye of sinful man thy glory may not see."

Faith Through Aging Eyes is not immune to the familiar question of the enemy, "Has God really said...?"

Has God really said He will never leave me nor forsake me?

Has God really said He will perfect that which concerns me?

Has God really said that His power is made perfect in my weakness? And if so, does this apply even when the weakness is due to aging?

How can I claim Psalm 112:7 as a promise that is demonstrated in my daily life?

As I prepare to sleep tonight, I am going to wrestle with this verse by reading the phrases in reverse order.

I am trusting in the Lord; therefore my heart is steadfast, and I have no fear of bad news!!!

How do you cope with the fear of bad news?

RAISING THE BAR

I made arrangements this week to meet one of our Senior Adult men at a residential facility where his wife is being cared for in her last stages of life with dementia. The facility was attractive. The staff was welcoming and kind.

I arrived a few minutes early so I was waiting when this distinguished gentleman walked in. He was pleased to see me and seemed proud to be able to introduce me to his wife. When the door to her locked unit was opened with a keypad, he said, "Oh, there she is, ready for us." I followed his lead and saw an elegant lady, well dressed and well groomed, seated by a table.

Her husband pulled out a chair for me, as I knew he would, and then went to the other side of the table. He said, "She expects me to be sitting on this side."

He grasped her hand and she grasped his. He tried several times to get her to respond to her name but she did not speak. She kept her eyes closed. He gently lifted her eyelids and they stayed open, but I am not sure that she saw anything.

He said that last week someone with a guitar sang "You

Are My Sunshine" and his wife sang along. I said, "Well, let's try to sing it." We did, and her mouth did try to form a few of the words.

This is the final inning of a 57-year marriage. I asked the husband if it was hard to visit. He said, "Coming to see her is the highlight of my week. I drive an hour to get here. I come every other day. When I leave I can't wait to get back."

When I told him he was a model of faithfulness, he referenced his vow.

Love plus vow yields an invincible commitment.

I asked if I could pray. When I did the wife sat motionless and the husband wept. I knew I was walking on Holy Ground as I quietly excused myself.

How, other than reminding us of our marriage vows, can this story impact our lives?

A RECEIPT FOR A PRAYER

I received an email telling me that a friend of mine and her ten-year-old daughter had chosen a personal scripture verse to use as a prayer for each of their family members and "others" who they knew needed prayer. I made the cut as one of the "others" and learned that they were praying for me from Ephesians 3:14-21.

Here is my receipt acknowledging that I have received this prayer and am claiming it for myself.

Father, I am so thankful that you have led my friend and her precious daughter to kneel before you and pray for me. I acknowledge you as the Name that we claim; the name that makes us brothers and sisters.

Thank you that out of your glorious riches you are strengthening me with power in my inner being. I need strength today. Thank you that your resources are more than I can measure and your desire to give is driven by your generous love.

Thank you for choosing to dwell in my heart. I want You to feel at home with me and for me to feel at home with You.

A RECEIPT FOR A PRAYER

Thank you that through the prayers of my friends I am being rooted and established in love and really getting a grip on how wide and long and high and deep Your love is.

This is almost too good to be true but I am choosing to believe that I am coming to know this Love that is much more than knowledge and that I am being filled up with you, God. I am glad that this verse says it is more than I can understand because I don't understand. I humbly receive and gratefully believe.

As I embrace this prayer, I am reminded that you are able to do so much more than I can ask or imagine and this power is at work within me now. I am grabbing on to this promise because I have some things that I don't even know how to talk to you about.

Take all the glory for Yourself, Father, and may generations praise you forever and ever.

This receipt acknowledges that I have received this prayer and claim the promises for myself.

Amen!!!

*L*ETTING GOD GET A WORD IN

We all have found ourselves in conversation with a person where we wonder if they will ever stop talking so we can get a word in. We are longing for dialogue but instead feel we are listening to a monologue.

I wonder if God feels that way when we pray.

We often go to prayer with an urgent list of needs that we want God to respond to in ways that we understand. It is like meeting with a friend and already knowing what you are going to say before the conversation begins.

There is a real place for this pattern of prayer and God is gracious in meeting us there. But, I would like to invite you to join me in a prayer pattern where we begin by sitting quietly with God and asking Him what He would like to talk about. Maybe He will surprise us by bringing to mind that which is in His heart that we have not noticed.

Maybe He will use what you have read in His word as the topic for your prayer.

One morning as I read John 13, I was reminded that when Jesus knew His time on earth was short, He ramped up His expression of love toward His disciples. It prompted me to pray that as seniors, we would use the chapters of our lives that we have left to be people who overflow with love more generously than ever before.

Are you listening to hear what the heart of God has to say to you?

RELEASING WHAT IS GONE

There is no doubt that aging involves loss. I have referenced processing loss as one of the essential ingredients to growing old gracefully. But how do we know when something is gone?

There is, of course, the loss that cannot be ultimately denied, such as the physical death of a loved one. Here the grieving process will protect by cushioning the impact with stages that lead to reality. When we first hear the news, we know it cannot be true, then time robs us of the comfort of denial. Gradually, we are compelled to acknowledge that what cannot be true is indeed true.

But there are other losses that have less tangible markers. It may be the loss of marital intimacy, as one spouse, in the riptide of dementia, is becoming a stranger. It may be the loss of being your own home repairman. Or reaching for something up high now produces pain and lifting heavy things is something you promise yourself you will not try again. It may be as simple as not being able to open the sealed bag in a box of cereal without reaching for the scissors.

It may be the loss of being recognized as a leader in your area of work. Someone else is now in the spotlight. There is a new experience of insecurity as you seek to get in step with the drumbeat of new leadership.

It may be an eroding of confidence that God will work in the lives of your children in the way you have prescribed for Him.

Whatever the loss, how do we access the grace to be diminished? Do we need to start by recognizing that the thing we are clinging to is gone?

My personal answer is "Yes," but the heart of Papa God has not ordained that the hand by which we release loss remains empty. When the hand of the person I love is no longer available to me, I find His hand drawing me deeper into His embrace.

There I learn to breathe again to the rhythm of His heart.

THE BEST AND WORST OF AGING

We had a 27-year-old guest at our senior adult prayer meeting today and the question was asked, "What is the best part of growing older and what is the worst?"

Among the answers for the best were, "freedom to say what you think," "not worrying about what people think," "being able to stay home in bad weather," "having a track record of God's faithfulness in our lives," and "knowing we are already living in eternity."

Among the answers for the worst were, "having our bodies betray us," "losing our balance," "hurting in places we didn't know we had," "having less energy," and "taking longer to do things."

An answer that could fit in either category was "not being able to remember."

What have you found to be the best and the worst part of growing older?

As I search for my answer, I am recognizing that the best part of aging is embracing my identity: I am not a product of my past, but rather a product of the cross!

I no longer want to write my own story. I want to take my hand off the pen and watch God script the last chapters of my life here on earth.

HOPE DRIES TEARS

When seeking to comfort a grieving friend, we remind ourselves that we do indeed grieve but NOT as those who have no hope. Grief is a place of brokenhearted loneliness. I am crushed with loneliness when I grieve because no one can experience my personal loss. I am the only one who really knows the complexity of what is gone.

The introduction of hope to the grieving heart must be carefully timed. Delivered too early, the hope described can sound like an abrasive cliché. Delivered too late, perceived hopelessness becomes a breeding ground for despair.

So, this is what I am asking from my friends:

Let me grieve—but not too long

Remind me of my hope—but not too early.

Walk with me and watch with me as hope dries tears.

How have you accessed the hope that is the anchor for your soul?

127

WHAT CRISIS REVEALS

I thought I understood crisis. I have taught the basics of crisis response for years. I have met with people in crisis and have been told that I have been helpful. But this crisis has torn through my mask of competence and revealed the shadows beneath it.

My best friend's house burned down this week. I was the only one in it when the fire started. I saw the raging flames on the deck towering over the height of the house. It looked to me like a war scene. The only thing I could think of was to save her two little pets. I ran to get them and carried them into the front yard. By then the neighbor had called 911 and people began to gather to look.

I don't know what they saw but I saw the dreams of my suffering friend going up in smoke. That very morning, she had let her tired and sore body rest in a lawn chair and said she was finally done. She had worked so hard and the house was now at a place where she could enjoy it. And within just a few hours, it had become a charred horror scene. The city gave us only ten days to demolish what was left of it.

Over the next few weeks, I realized I had defaulted to unhealthy ways of expressing my pain. I did not spend long periods of time in prayer. I did not run to search my Bible for comfort. I did not confide in my friends. I was impatient with my husband, my sister, and most anyone who called to ask how I was and what they can do.

I couldn't think of what they could do.

I was sad that I did not have a story that brought glory to my God, but rather one that revealed there is much of His work that still needs to be done in me.

My prayer became, "Father, forgive ME for I know not what I do."

*T*ENSES OF GRATITUDE

Aging is a fertile field for past tense gratitude. I can reflect on my life and recognize God's protective hand on my childhood years. How does a child even stay alive on a small farm where my small hands were the only ones available to do what would be a challenge to a skilled technician?

Do memories of my teen years and early adulthood make God shudder as much as I do in retrospect? What about the time I got our 1950 Ford up to 100 miles per hour and won the drag race with my high school competitor, who was a boy. Were the angels tired?

What about the risks from nursing school where we slipped our names to the business men who came to "take us out on a date" because our nearly blind house mother wouldn't let us go unless the men knew our names?

Then we can move from protective grace to provisional grace. How can it be that I was trusted to be the children's pastor of a mega church? I stepped forward when the need presented because our senior pastor had taught me that availability was more important than ability. I spent the next decade watching God do what He has promised, "The one who calls you is faithful, and He will do it." (1 Thessalonians 5:24 NIV)

I remember needing 600 Sunday School teachers every fall. We started with a blank flip chart and every year we got the 600 names. Some of the parents thought I was amazing. I tried to tell them that it was God who is amazing, but not everyone can process this mystery. It did give me the courage to push our volunteers past their comfort zone as I knew that once you experience God doing through you what you could never do, you will never leave ministry or deny a miracle.

This same God of the impossible has provided senior adult stories that I will continue to record and tell. But for today, I can, in faith, lean on the God who has been faithful. Jesus Christ is the same yesterday, today, and forever. (Hebrews 13:8)

What about the future tense of faith? How will I embrace the losses of aging? How do I demonstrate the "grace to be diminished" when the one who is being diminished is me?

Please God, may my gratitude attitude cover past, present, and future tenses. May I, in faith, thank you now that Jesus Christ is the same, yesterday, today, and tomorrow. May I lean hard on the promise that His power is made perfect in weakness, even when the weakness is due to aging.

How are you processing the losses of aging? Are you able to trust the God who has been faithful to be faithful? Tell your stories of God's faithfulness to others, trusting these stories will nurture the faith of those who hear.

POLISHING THE REARVIEW MIRROR

I sat in a prayer group this week led by a senior adult lady who is struggling with weakness. Some days it is hard for her to hold her head up. She walks into the building leaning on a walker on wheels and stops every few feet to catch her breath.

This leader went around the circle and asked each of us for our personal prayer requests. When her turn came, she said she was just so filled with joy and thanksgiving. She attributed this to learning that two members of our younger staff team were pregnant. It prompted memories for her of how she loved being pregnant and how thankful she was for the wonderful life she had been given.

What do you polish your rearview mirror with in order to see these memories, even when your path today is difficult to navigate?

There is an old hymn that goes something like this: "Hast thou not seen? All thy desires have been granted in what He ordaineth." I am delighted when I am given insight to see that the awkward place I find myself in at any given time can be traced to a desire I have guarded in my heart.

Faith Through Aging Eyes enables gazing in the rearview mirror. It is often in that mirror that God's knowing me intimately and planning for me intricately is revealed.

I have seen God's faithfulness expressed in His plan for my life today. May it strengthen my faith in the dimly lit path of tomorrow, knowing that the Hand that has crafted the past will not grow weary.

Moving

There is something exciting about moving to a new house. Every circumstance is different, of course, but if your old house burned down, it means you get to buy a new toothbrush and a new couch, as well as everything in between.

If you are an artist, which I am not, it means going to a furniture store and picturing how everything will look in the new house. If you feel responsible for the practical, which I do, you check in regularly with your real estate broker, compare the amount in the insurance checks with the amount needed for closing, and think about what else might go wrong.

There is also something distressing about moving to a new house. You find things are dirty that you thought would have been clean. I wonder why I am so comfortable with my own mess and so distressed by someone else's. You find things broken that you didn't expect. You take the short trip to crazy because you can't find the thing you need. You have everything but the one thing you need NOW.

There is a kind of grief in not being in a familiar place, a place where you have memories.

I cannot escape the reality of aging being a diminishing experience in many ways, including my environment. It is probable that I will downsize to a smaller house, maybe even a condo. Later it could be an apartment, assisted living, nursing home, bed, and finally a box.

It is with this stark reality I praise God that I dwell in the secret place of the Most High!

I'm thankful, I'm excited, I'm scared, and I'm tired, but most of all I am forever grateful for a never-changing God in an ever-changing world.

CONFUSED AND FORGETFUL

These two words are nightmare terms for us as we age. We try to make them funny. I have a mug that says, "I think I may be confused but maybe I am not." And then I have a keychain attached to an 8 x 10 plastic mat imprinted with "These are the keys I haven't lost yet."

Confusion and forgetfulness have become such dreaded companions to aging that we think they are the price to be paid for a long life. I was reminded recently that we, who see *Faith Through Aging Eyes*, do not have exclusive rights to these experiences.

I was invited to speak to a group of young mothers. One mother was there with what looked like a big scarf draped around her neck. As I looked closer, I could see it was actually a sling that held a six-day-old baby. Other mothers came pushing strollers or holding toddlers on one hip while balancing a plate of muffins and fruit with the other hand. What surprised me most was how confused and forgetful most of them seemed to be.

They asked what group they had been in last week because they couldn't remember. The instructions for the morning schedule had to be repeated in order to be understood. The attempt to give directions for finding a room was so unsuccessful that one of the leaders said, "I will just lead you there."

No one in the young Mom's group seemed to be concerned about this forgetfulness and confusion. I think they would have labeled their experience "life." Why is it not simply "life" for those of us who are aging?

I want to strip my next encounter with confusion and forgetfulness of the fear that it is happening because of my age. I want to laugh at *and* with myself.

Maybe it is true that it takes me longer to find a memory because I have more to sort through.

Children think Grandmas and Grandpas are fun.

I agree. I think I'm fun too!!!

*F*ROM SIGNIFICANCE TO SERENITY

Several years ago a popular book subtitled "Changing Your Game Plan from Success to Significance" challenged readers to release the tyranny of success and embrace something of significance. The title *Half Time* identified the intended reader.

It was like rain on a parched land for those whose apparent success felt meaningless. Many chose to earn less money and hold a less prestigious position in order to invest in something that would improve the lives of others and advance the causes of justice.

In reflecting on this paradigm shift, I wonder if there is a season where we are called to move from significance to serenity. If so, it raises many questions. Who is initiating the transition? Is it personally chosen? Is it imposed by aging, employment, or relational transitions?

How each of us is able to personally answer these questions contributes to whether serenity is a welcome gift or an elusive goal. We know that godliness with contentment is great gain. Paul said that he had learned to be content without the advantage of circumstances.

How do we process the losses of significance in ways that build a bridge to serenity?

GLIMPSES OF GLORY

Most days seem to run their course and, if anyone would ask us to report the highlights, we would sort through the routines looking for something interesting to tell. But there are times when there are breakthrough moments where we become aware that there is an alignment between the desires of our heart and the reality of our experience.

The old hymn writer puts it this way, "Hast thou not seen how all thy longings have been granted in what He ordaineth?" When we get a glimpse of our experiences actually being that for which we have longed, rather than something with which to cope, we are moved to worship. May God open our eyes to these glimpses of His glory.

When we find a thread in our life that doesn't seem to have a purpose, may we trust that it is being woven into a story yet to be revealed. May our glimpses of glory give us courage to praise and resound to the praise of His glory.

GOD IS PAYING ATTENTION

We had a first time attendee in our prayer group this week; a middle-aged man with prophetic gifts. The group is led by a grandmother in her 80s. This grandmother poured out her heart's concern regarding her grandson giving an engagement ring this Christmas to a girl who is not yet a disciple of Jesus Christ. As prayers continued to be verbalized, the newcomer remained with head bowed and silent. At one point, the grandmother leader thanked God for this new attendee and then tenderly asked God to pay special attention to his prayers.

At the end of the prayer time, the new attendee told the grandmother leader that during this hour he had been silently praying for her grandson and girlfriend. God had given him a picture of this girlfriend coming to faith in Jesus Christ and being powerfully used in the Kingdom of God. Just as this new attendee was thanking God for this promise revealed, the grandmother prayed that God would pay special attention to the prayers of this man.

Our God is paying attention and weaving our prayers. We bow in humble gratitude for the adventure of prayer.

I WANT TO HEAR "WELL DONE!"

How can I be sure that the life I am living will one day allow me to hear "Well done" from Jesus? I know that my salvation is all of His grace so I am not concerned about that. I know some people think I have amazing patience and err on the side of grace. I am not confident that their opinion has much validity. I know some people think I err on the side of having no boundaries and let people use me in a way that is of no benefit to them or me. I am not confident that their opinion has much validity either.

My mentor in ministry pointed me to this practice: "Sum up at night what thou hast done by day. And in the morning what thou hast to do. Dress and undress thy soul. Mark the decay and growth of it." (George Herbert)

But how do I measure decay and growth?

In *Simply Jesus*, N.T. Wright uses these words when explaining the Passover meal Jesus celebrated with His disciples before His death: "This is how the presence of Jesus is to be known among His followers. Sacrifice and presence."

What if I were to measure my day by evidence of sacrifice and presence?

I would not get much applause from the crowds and there would be no postcards to send from my vacation.

But would the angels be celebrating? Would Jesus be recognized as my reigning King? Would I have joy simply because the One Who loves me has promised that when I commit my way to Him, He will give me the desires of my heart?

*L*OW VISIBILITY

We walk by faith and not by sight, yet there are times when I am reminded that I am still looking to see some assurance that God will show me His mercy. Is it an oxymoron to say that my faith is experiencing low visibility?

I remember a time in Bolivia many years ago. I was a nurse and had accompanied a physician and a small team to teach some basic health screening skills to the missionaries of some nomadic jungle tribes.

On the morning we were to fly into one of the sites, the area was covered with dense fog. We waited to hear from air traffic control that it was safe to fly. I didn't really get ready because I knew that the pilot couldn't possibly see and the small plane had no instruments. To my amazement, we were told we could go.

The plane was packed and since I was the smallest person, I was placed in the back, sitting on some duffel bags. After a time in the air, I heard the pilot say to the doctor, "There are mountains on both sides of us, and I can't see."

I curled up and cried, certain we were all going to die.

Then I heard the pilot say, "It's okay now. I can see."

Our plane grazed over the landing strip to clear it of the cattle then we circled back and landed. Our missionary hosts and a gathering of children, who were fascinated by my blonde hair and wanted to touch it, greeted us. I was glad to have them touching me but most fascinated by hearing the missionary say, "We tried to radio you this morning and tell you not to come because of the fog, but we couldn't get through. So we prayed. When we heard the sound of your engine coming through the valley between the two mountains, suddenly the fog lifted right at the place where your plane broke through."

I was not scared for another moment during that entire trip.

I am scared tonight. I cannot see. I am going to pray. I am going to expect the fog to lift right at the place and time needed.

AN UNEXPECTED CONVERSATION

The following record of a conversation between my mother and me is an example of how we learned to talk to each other when she was diagnosed with severe dementia and needed help with basic physical care and astute supervision. She lived a year after this event.

I learned not to try to correct everything she said and tried to make it fun. I recognize that all of this was possible because I was granted the gift of a friend who carried the heavy load of personal care for Mom.

I remember the following conversation between my mom and I as my friend, Mom's nurse, was giving her a sponge bath. As she was routinely getting Mom ready for the day, Mom said, "I'll be clean when I get to heaven."

"Are you planning on going to heaven?"

"Yes, I'm going tonight."

"Are you glad?"

"Yes, aren't you?"

"Well, I'll miss you."

"I won't miss you. I'll be in heaven. I'll see Daddy there."

"Will you tell him I miss him?"

"Sure."

"Well, I hope you have a nice trip."

"Jesus will carry me in His arms."

"Do you want to go naked or do you want to wear something?"

"I'll go naked because I'll get a beautiful robe when I get there."

"Okay."

"Brrrrrrr!"

"Would you like to wear something down here so you won't be so cold until Jesus gets here?"

"Yes, I think that would be a good idea."

What have you learned from people with dementia? Can you identify the caregivers sent from God?

*T*HERE IS SOMEONE HOME

Most of us have heard the crude remark "The lights are on but nobody's home" referring to someone with cognitive impairment. I recently found myself in conversation with a person whom, I have since learned, has a known diagnosis of dementia. As we talked, it became increasingly clear to me that there was little relationship between my comments and the responses I was hearing, yet the person I was talking to seemed to be enjoying the exchange of words.

I caught myself pondering, "Why am I engaging in this conversation?"

Here are some things I considered that day.

Is lending dignity to a person by listening to them an expression of love?

Am I able to be content, for a time, simply honoring the person for who he or she is without assessing what value the conversation has for me?

Could the person I am talking with feel the benefit of human contact even if it cannot be expressed in coherent words?

Do we have any examples of conversation that bridges cognitive barriers?

I wonder why God invites us to talk to Him when our thoughts are not His thoughts.

Does He listen to me when I don't get it, simply because He loves me and wants to strengthen our relationship?

Does He know that I benefit from a conversation with Him even when my responses are not yet lined up with His intentions?

Does He like to hear my voice because He loves me rather than because He needs me to contribute to His knowledge base?

BARREN WALLS, BLOSSOMING HEART

I wanted to visit my friend in her home one last time before she moved to a senior living facility with supportive services. This home, from which she will soon move, has the fragrance of a sanctuary for me and for many others. Countless prayers have been heard by these walls. Countless stories have been confided in this place, knowing the walls **could not** talk and the listener **would not** talk to anyone except God.

There was an unfamiliar dread in my own heart as I drove toward this visit. It was a strange thing to experience because it was replacing the joyful anticipation of spending time in a friendship I have learned to cherish. I asked myself why this was hard for me. I reminded myself that I had made this same trip for the better part of 40 years.

My visits to this home began when I sought counsel for my own confused and broken heart. I was gently but firmly pointed to God's Word as it was applied to my life with the wisdom of one who knows how to hold grace and truth in tension. Later the visits became more of a mentoring relationship as I was trusted with ministry responsibilities.

I valued the security of a safe place to talk and someone who would ask me hard questions, holding the bar high. I sometimes told others that this friend "drilled in my teeth" but I met with her as often as I could because I knew I was loved, and I also knew that I and those I love were being prayed for.

In recent years, though counseling and mentoring still happen, our time together is more characterized by friendship. I smile as she calls me her pastor and friend, knowing she is genuine in this description but also knowing how generous God has been to make this true.

As I arrived at the familiar modest home, the door flew open and my name was called with the tone of someone who was glad I was there. As we settled into the now sparsely furnished room, my eyes scanned the barren walls that had once been covered with cherished pieces of art. Most of the wall décor would prompt a story of its origin and meaning. I stated the obvious thing to my friend and said, "There is nothing on your walls." She agreed that this was true.

It didn't take me long to realize that even though the walls were barren, the heart of my friend was blossoming. She bubbled over with joy as she talked about the kindness and love that was being poured out on her and her beloved husband by their children. She described what their new place would be like and assured me I would love it there.

She testified to the footprints she had detected in her life events that she knew were arranged by God. She spoke with strength of His revealing Himself to her.

At one point when she rose from her chair, she acknowledged some dizziness. She grabbed her walker just to be safe. This physical weakness confirmed that the move was a good thing. It's also a good thing that weakness is undetectable in her spiritual and emotional journey.

As I had come to expect, she asked me what God had been teaching me, and with excitement opened her Bible to the verses I referenced, declaring she had never seen that in the scripture before. At almost 88 years old, having devoured the Bible for most of these years, she was allowing the Living Word to speak new things.

As we prayed together, the blossoms in her heart released a familiar fragrance. The friend who knows me and loves me anyway will have a new address, but her heart will not have a new home. The fragrance I thought I would miss was not coming from the now barren walls but from the heart that is at home with Jesus.

I drove away looking forward to our next visit, eager to see how the new walls will be decorated and eager to encounter the heart whose home is eternal.

MY SON CAME HOME!

Her radiant face spoke more loudly than the words that flowed. "It was 8:30 in the morning when the doorbell rang. I couldn't imagine who would be at our house at that time. I opened the door and there stood my son!"

Does anything bring more joy to a mother than for one of her children to arrive unannounced on Mother's Day weekend? Or any other weekend for that matter.

It could have been a tough weekend for this mother. Her own mother had died less than a year prior and this son was many states away serving in military duty while her daughter was on another continent.

But all potential sadness faded when she saw the face of her son. He had come home and he would be spending the weekend with her.

Can we borrow this picture and remind ourselves that God loves us so much that He is delighted when we plan to spend time with Him, sacrifice something else in order to be with Him, tell Him the things that are too big or too little to tell to anyone else? Just sit and listen as He talks to us?

Let's just show up and catch God's smile!

WHAT ARE YOU COUNTING TODAY?

We have a wonderful couple who has been faithful in our prayer group for years. Six months ago the man developed some health problems that needed to be attended to either in the hospital or in-home medical care.

In the weeks that followed, several from the group would bring an encouraging report of this friend's progress. "He is getting better." "It is healing slowly." "They will be back soon."

The optimistic reports proved true, except that when one thing would get better, another health challenge presented. For six months if it hasn't been one thing it has been another.

Being sick these days is a fulltime job. Life becomes all about making and keeping medical appointments. Just when recovery seems in sight, another surgery is necessary.

I called this man's wife to tell her I missed them and how sorry I was for the long, hard bumpy road. She answered the phone with the lilting, joyful voice I have known and loved for years. She seemed to be almost laughing as she talked.

"Oh, we're doing just great! After 85 years of good health, we now have caught up with six months of illness. We are so blessed. All you have to do is look around those hospitals and you realize how blessed you are!"

When I asked if they would be back soon, she said, "I hope so, but we have another month of one doctor after another." (More laughter.)

Reflecting on this conversation, I wonder what I am counting. Am I counting my blessings today or only lamenting my losses?

THE BOUNDARY LINES

I love the theme of Psalm 16 that says the boundary lines have fallen for me in pleasant places. Surely I have a delightful inheritance.

It reminds me that in this life there are boundaries that guide us, protect us and sometimes set limits for us that need to be respected.

By nature, we want to push past these boundaries, or at the very least, ensure that no one imposes on or pushes through them.

My friend recently bought a new home. Part of its charm was the beautifully landscaped yard. I felt concern when I saw a surveyor mark up the property with orange paint, indicating that the boundary lines were about ten feet closer to the house than the previous owner had indicated.

When I told my friend about this, she said, "Good, then there is less for us to mow." When the owner of the adjacent lot said he would be cutting down the trees on this strip of questionable ownership, my friend responded, "Just make sure they fall your way."

I want to embrace this response and make it my own. I don't need to protect every square inch of my physical or emotional land.

I have a delightful inheritance.

TELL ME THE STORY AGAIN

Yesterday my five-year-old granddaughter came to visit me in my office. I had some paper and markers ready for her. She printed my name, which is Besta to her. I am amazed at how fast she is moving from being a baby to becoming a little girl. As she sat on her mother's lap, my memories took me back to the days when her mother was my co-worker.

When this co-worker learned that she was going to have a baby, she began planning to be a stay-at-home mom. I was feeling sad that we would not be working together, but also excited that she would be a mother. As we talked about how this would all be, we decided that since the real grandmother lived in Australia, I could "adopt" this baby as my grandchild. We decided to call me Besta, which is Grandma in Norwegian.

I went along to the ultrasound appointment and saw my precious little girl being knit together in her mother's womb. One day, about halfway through the pregnancy, there was a little note taped to my office door. It said, "Good night, Besta. I love you."

I decided to tell this story to my granddaughter yesterday. I told her that her daddy and mommy had prayed for a baby and then she started to grow inside her mommy's tummy. I said that when she was still living in her mommy's tummy, she had written me a note.

On hearing this, her eyes grew big and her face reflected delight. "Besta," she said, "will you tell me that story again?" Nothing pleased me more than to tell it again and let her revel in the knowledge that she was planned for and wanted.

I need these reminders for myself. I am thankful that prayer is both talking and listening. When I listen to God, He reminds me that He thought carefully about how to make me and knit me together in my mother's womb (see Psalm 139). He made me because He wanted me to be in His family and to call Him Abba, Father. I am one of a kind, and that makes me precious to Him.

He never tires of my asking, "Abba! Tell me the story again."

PRAYER CHANGES PRAYER

I had come to the home of my 91-year-old friend to put the finishing touches on his memorial service. He has been accepted as a hospice patient, and knowing that the health care system has exhausted its resources for treatment, he has chosen quality of life. His strong faith in the hope of spending eternity with Jesus makes talking about death easy.

In planning the service, we discussed favorite hymns, the scripture he wanted read, who would bring words of remembrance and what I should talk about when bringing a message of hope.

We laughed together when he said that after the service, "we" could take the ashes to Illinois and spread them on a gravesite he owned there. I couldn't just let that go so I asked if it would be "we" who would take the ashes. Allowing the reality to settle in, he said, "No, I won't be going."

Having taken care of the details, I looked at this man through the eyes of my experience as a registered nurse and said, "I am not at all sure that you can lean hard on the expectation that your death is imminent. Of course you could die before I leave today, but then so could I." Pondering this I asked him, "I wonder if you need to be prepared to live as well as be prepared to die."

He then acknowledged that the doctors had also thought he may actually be improving. We sat together quietly before he told me he had changed his language of prayer. For two weeks he had begged God to let him die. "Lord, I've had enough. I'd like you to help me slip away in the dark of night." But then he remembered that Jesus Himself had prayed, "If possible, take this away from me."

The memory of Jesus and His trial helped my friend understand that the Lord had not turned His back on him. "It's just that God wasn't ready." So the new prayer language is, "I'm ready when you are. You call me and I will come." Explaining further, he turned to me and said, "There's no use pushing Him as He's not a pushover." He concluded with, "I'll go when He calls me and not before."

May that be our prayer too.

No MORE PATCHES

It seemed normal in our childhood for someone to patch a worn piece of clothing so that its use could be extended. Today, we only see patches on new clothing as a fashion statement.

It seemed normal in our childhood to take a broken thing to a repair shop so it could be fixed. Today, even if you can find someone who knows how to fix things, it is often more expensive to repair than to buy a new one.

We have learned to view everything as designed for temporary use. Everything, that is, except our bodies. Even though the Bible clearly teaches that our bodies are tents designed for temporary use, there is something within us that is driven to patch it one more time.

How do we know when medical efforts have been maximized and further treatment will have no benefit? The medical community is hesitant to make this decision. Doctors live under the pressure of legal liability. They also struggle to maintain the image we have imposed upon them, that of having a patch that will keep our tent from leaking or collapsing altogether.

It is only a culture of prayerful dependence that will set us free to yield to the inevitable "let's not patch this anymore" and transfer the expiration date of the tent to the One who made it.

I am grateful for the models I have had, who have utilized all medical means but when all have been exhausted, have been able to say "Enough is enough."

Several years ago I heard Professor Stan Hauerwas say that most Christians die as practical atheists. This was said in the context of acting as though the end of life in these tents is the end of life.

Let's pray for each other that we may demonstrate that the end of life in these tents sets us free to be swallowed up by life. Then, when medical intervention has exhausted its effectiveness, we will be free to say, "No more patches."

MY LUNCH TODAY

We have stories in the Bible of God asking people to bring what they have to Him and then He takes the scraps we bring and does a miracle. One example of this is the story of Jesus feeding the five thousand. If it were my task to feed that many people, it would not occur to me to ask for a little boy's lunch so I could get started. Clearly Jesus did not need the lunch.

One of the conundrums of aging is the increased frequency of being expected to do the impossible. It can be as simple as remembering an essential detail or as complex as trusting God for the salvation of one who is desperately loved. It can be that we are driven to seek justice for a person, relieve suffering, or bring hope. It might be as practical as providing food and shelter for someone hungry and homeless.

Is there a pattern in the story of Jesus feeding the five thousand that I can follow? Is it possible that my part is to bring my lunch and His part is to do the impossible? If so, what is my lunch? What do I have that I can bring?

I am learning, when I hear a crushing story, to ask God to

help me understand what my part is in this particular story. Today my part seems to be prayer and availability. If my phone rings, I will answer it. If I am asked to come, I will go. While I wait, I will pray.

What do you have for lunch today? If Jesus needs it, will you give it to Him?

Maybe I Can Bring a Smile

A friend of mine is in the process of aligning her income to her lifestyle. If being a Senior Adult were an academy, she would be in preschool. In other words, she is younger than I am.

A few weeks ago she accepted an offer on her "for sale" condo. In this market, you are glad to break even, and she is. So now where does she move? She told me that she was considering an apartment in a Senior Living Center. Because this particular place is where we have significant ministry, my immediate response was, "Maybe this is your mission field?"

With refreshing honesty my friend confided to me that the environment of the Senior Living Center did not feel like a "fit." She would have much preferred a duplex with young families nearby yet she feels this Senior Living Center is where God is leading her. She has come to understand that this will not be her "home." She knows that she is dwelling in Jesus and the journey is her home.

I often sign my letters to Senior Adults, "Thank you for the privilege of being your pastor as you continue to be my teacher." I am thankful for this teacher. She concluded our conversation by saying, "Maybe I can bring a smile?"

Where is your mission field? Are you bringing a smile?

*L*OOK UP AND ENJOY THE FEAST

A big jar of cashews slipped out of my hand and the nuts scattered across the kitchen floor. As I was brushing them into the dustpan, I wondered if I should just pick them up with my fingers and eat them. It seemed wasteful to throw them out. Then I remembered the bird and squirrel feeding station I watch every morning while I am having my coffee. I walked barefooted across the deck, stepping over remnants of birdseed, and spread the cashews along the rail.

Before long a small squirrel arrived on the deck. He groveled through the remnants of seed then sat straight up with his head in the air. It seemed he had noticed something.

I silently talked to him. "Look up. There's something special on the rail."

He walked to the post but I couldn't tell if he was going to jump down or hop up.

"Look up!" I said again.

To my delight he scrambled up the post and found himself in the middle of a pile of cashews. He tasted one and was

169

absolutely hooked. Chewing as fast as he could, he devoured mouthful after mouthful. When he couldn't eat anymore, he stuffed his mouth full of cashews and ran off to hide them. Not too much later, he came back and ran off with more.

Do I realize that a table has been prepared for me today? Am I looking up and feasting?

IT'S NOT BECAUSE HE DOESN'T CARE

My cell phone made the sound that lets me know I have a message. As I listened I found myself hoping I was misunderstanding what I was hearing. But, as I listened again, there was no denying that my friend was on her way to the emergency room at the heart hospital.

She had gone to Urgent Care because of dizziness and the information they had gathered there pointed to a heart problem. In the message she told me not to come, but as her reality settled into my mind, my hands were reaching for my car keys.

I found her in an ER room looking healthy but with a heart monitor recording her rhythm, an IV dripping and oxygen flowing. She had already had a CT scan and was waiting for results. Her daughter, who is a young adult, was sitting with her.

After a brief update and prayer, I asked her where her husband was. Her daughter said he was at home. She said she had called him and he said he would probably take a shower. Trying to hang this in the best possible light, I reminded the daughter that cell phones don't work in ER rooms so he probably had tried to call.

My friend, in a tone of deep confidence and intimate knowing, said, "It's not because he doesn't care."

Thankfully, the test results of this ER work-up revealed good news. No heart issues were found. But I left having been challenged by my friend's trust in her husband's care and her acceptance of his not showing up. She knows who he is and she doesn't measure his caring by prescribed expectations.

I want to honor God in the same way my friend honored her husband.

God may not be meeting my expectations based on what I want Him to do today but this I know: IT IS NOT BECAUSE HE DOESN'T CARE!!

God grant me the grace to rest in this truth.

FRESH FOOTPRINTS IN FRESH SNOW

Everything outside is pure white. The ground is covered with snow. The pine trees have their green needles wearing white shawls while a red cardinal positions himself for a stunning portrait. When I was a child in the country, the snow stayed white. Here in the suburbs we know that this time of purity is short so we cherish these moments.

Something ran across our entire yard during the night. I can follow the trail from my window. If I were to walk out, I could tell if it was a deer, a rabbit, a raccoon, or a fox by the footprints, the weight, and the pattern of movement.

I am reminded that I, too, am making footprints. Footprints can look one way from a distance. Closer examination will reveal more.

The eyes of the Lord do not miss a step. Others also may be watching and weighing my movements against my words.

May God grant us grace to allow Him to direct our path in such a pattern that those who follow will be led to the heart of the One Who made us and gives us reason to run.

*F*ACE TO FACE

I combed my hair today before I tried to connect with my friend on FaceTime. This was important because FaceTime is a feature of an iPad that lets you see the person you are talking to. What's more concerning to me is that it also lets me see myself. It's kind of like a living mirror.

If someone had told me 60 years ago, when we had a party line and our phone number was 4F2211, the technological advances that were coming, I don't think I would have believed them. Our number, 4F2211, meant that when the wall phone rang with two short rings and two long rings, someone was calling us. The phone was busy quite a lot because there were several combinations of rings on each line. There was also limited privacy as anyone could pick up at anytime and listen in your conversation. Our one neighbor had asthma so it was always easy to know when she was listening in.

One ring would connect to the operator, who was a real person and knew everything about everybody's life. The operator could be reached when there was an emergency or if we wanted to break into a conversation that was taking too long.

We did eventually get private lines. And even though the phone numbers changed, we still had to be home to get the call or to make a call to someone else.

Answering machines came next. Now, if someone wasn't home, you could leave a message and they could call you back.

Then came cell phones. These could ride in your pocket or purse. Anyone could call you at any time if you had prepaid minutes or a monthly call plan.

Smart phones quickly followed. These keep your calendar, your emails, check the weather, get breaking news, and take pictures.

As if that wasn't enough, now the FaceTime iPad lets you see who you are talking to.

Does it work to trace this progression and apply it to intimacy in prayer?

Do we begin by learning corporate prayers that are somewhat rote and usually guarded?

Do we move to a more personal and private conversation with God but isolate it to specific times?

Is the next phase one where prayer is an anytime, all-day conversation?

Am I wanting now to hear God's voice and see His face, somehow like wanting to learn how to use FaceTime?

Face time with God is something we desire when we are assured of our identity. If I am really unconditionally loved by God, I don't have to edit my prayers.

Knowing who I am in His sight prompts me to listen for His voice. I don't fear condemnation but know I will receive absolute acceptance.

I am learning to listen before I talk in prayer. A phone call is only meaningful if both parties are on the same subject and communicating with one another. I want to learn to interact with Jesus and let Him choose the topic.

Prayer is boring when I'm the only one talking.

A PRAYER FOR A STEADFAST STORY

(written in reflection of a class reunion)

Our Father in heaven, my heart is filled with worship. I am especially grateful today for your story. You created us to walk with you, but we decided to cut our own path. Then you created a way back through faith in your Son, our Lord Jesus Christ. After He died for our disobedience, He rose in resurrection power. Now Your Holy Spirit is released to live in us.

Our eternal journey with you begins here on earth. In your grace, you have written a personal story for each of us. You have knit us together in our mother's womb and numbered our days. You have designed a course that advances Your Kingdom. You have uniquely equipped each of us to run the race marked out for us. This means you have written a story for me to live out!

After a weekend of class reunion celebration, I thought a lot about my story. Its beginnings. Its twists and turns. Its joy and pain.

Father, I want to tell you I am sorry for the many times I have outlined the next chapter without reading your script; for the many times I have been discontented, wanting a different plot line with different characters.

I realize that like everyone in my age group, I have more history than I have future. I want this time of reflection to be a turning point where I choose to stick more carefully to the story Jesus has written for me, allowing Him to make me aware of when I delete from or add to His script.

Father, from this day forward, I want my history to be His Story. Heavenly Father, thank you for writing a story for me. Holy Spirit, come be my editor. I pray in your name and for your sake, Jesus.

Amen!

A PROMISE-KEEPING GOD

From time to time, I go back and read in my old Amplified Bible. Many of the verses have dates written in the margin. I have always enjoyed the amplifications of words, giving various possible meanings.

I recently noticed something new. Note the reference to age in the following passage:

Who satisfies your mouth (your necessity and desire at your personal age) with good; so that your youth, renewed, is like the eagle's (strong, overcoming, soaring)! (Psalm 103:5 Amplified)

Does God satisfy us differently when we are old than He did when we were young? Does He add more spice because our taste buds are tired? Does He serve smaller portions? Does He give us more time to chew?

I found a translation that was even more specific to "old age."

Who satisfieth thine old age with good [things]; thy youth is renewed like the eagle's. (Psalm 103:5 DARBY)

Darby published his first translation in the 1860s. He makes this comment on his latest work published in 1890: "In the issue of this translation, the purpose is not to offer to the man of letters a learned work, but rather to provide the simple and unlearned reader with as exact a translation as possible."

Let's take joy in this today as we celebrate *Faith Through Aging Eyes*. God has a designated menu for seniors. He is giving us what we need, which is really the same as what we want, and as we allow Him to feed us, we are becoming strong "overcomers" who soar on wings like eagles.

He is a promise-keeping God!!!

*T*HE SPECTACULAR COLOR SHOW

When you plan a weather-dependent event and the elements cooperate perfectly, you may be asked if you had placed a special order requesting these conditions. This was my experience as we held our Senior Adult Prayer Retreat at a local nature center.

A gentle breeze encouraged the shedding of leaves as the sun reflected the blazing glory of the autumn colors. The temperature and humidity were perfect for walking the trails and eating a picnic lunch.

Our prayer and praise sessions were held in a comfortable room with glass walls. It was quite natural to acknowledge our Creator and marvel at His work.

As I lead from a podium in the center of the room, I recognize that most of the participants are in the autumn of their lives. Most are familiar with grief and acquainted with suffering. Many left the comforts of a known environment to join me for the adventure of a day together listening to God. We celebrate God speaking to us through His work, His world, His works, and His whispers.

Many of our physical bodies are evidencing the wear and

tear of years. The Bible tells us that outwardly we are wasting away, yet that is not our focus. Faces are glowing with the joy of worship. Tears are gently shed as the Holy Spirit breathes on hearts.

We stand amazed that our Creator is genuinely interested in talking to us and listening. The created world is showcased by the care and nurture of the nature center staff but the hearts of those who have known the loving care of Jesus are showcased as they worship.

The whole earth is ablaze with His Glory!!!!

BECOMING A CATALYST FOR QUESTIONS

Faith Through Aging Eyes gives us the vantage point of seeing things through the lens of experience. We want to give advice that will prevent an unwelcome outcome to a chosen path. Well-meaning as we are, we usually find unsolicited advice to be perceived as criticism. Then there is what we see as an answer that has served us well. We want to give another person the benefit of our wisdom. But what is this person's question? If he has no question, our answer will fall on deaf ears.

How do we live in such a way that we become a catalyst for questions?

This becomes a heart-wrenching challenge when the answer we are aching to give our loved one is how loved they are by God. We have found an effective model of how this can work in ministry when church outreach partners with a government program.

Our local county Department of Aging had identified residents that were totally alone. No one visited them as they had burned all their bridges to other people. Once we learned about this, as a Senior Adult Ministry, we wanted to visit these abandoned ones. When asked why, we said, "Because that is where Jesus would go."

Respecting the separation of church and state protocol, we agreed not to go with a primary agenda of evangelism. Instead, we proposed that we would go and ACT like Jesus until the person we visited would ASK why we kept coming even when we were not given a warm welcome. Only then would we TELL.

There is no law against answering a question, even when the answer is your own statement of faith.

Yes, Jesus is the Answer! But what is the question?

MAKE TIME YOUR FRIEND

I am looking at my little pine tree. I captured this treasure from the wooded area of my friend's farm in the days following his premature death. I wanted something living to protect the memories of our precious times together.

Today the little tree is bearing the weight of heavy snow. Its posture is determined by its encasement in ice. Everything in me wants to brush the snow off and melt the ice, but I know this little tree would not survive this "tender loving care."

I need to make time my friend, waiting for the sun to shine, the temperatures to warm, and then let the little tree stretch forth its own branches.

Maybe you feel like this tree today when everyone else is celebrating. Maybe this tree looks like one of your loved ones. Maybe everything in you wants your spouse back, your broken relationship healed, or your health restored.

I listened to a message yesterday entitled "Nothing Just Happens" by T. D. Jakes. The whole message is "nothing just happens." We are part of a bigger story—God's story.

I invite you to join me in making time our friend.

STANDING ON THE PROMISES

One of my favorite Bibles is at least 40 years old. It is an Amplified version that I have been able to have rebound. I have decided to use it for my regular reading and studying in 2014. It will be fun to compare what I thought worth underlining in 1974, at the age of 30, with what I want to underline this year.

I know God's promises have not changed!

Back in 1974 I claimed these promises. I wonder if, back then, I said Amen to the promises that were evident to me in my experiences with God.

This year I will claim these promises again. Today I want to say Amen to them because I am confident in the One Who made them.

This will be full circle to my childhood faith where my trust was without borders. I am now waking up every morning to *Oceans* by Hillsong United. When we live by *Faith Through Aging Eyes*, we become familiar with "where feet may fail," and even more familiar with "in oceans deep, my faith will stand."

Stand with me on all of God's Promises!!!

*F*OLLOWING JESUS TO THE FINISH LINE

She always wheels halfway into the hallway so she can watch me walk away. When I get to the corner, I turn and wave. There is one more hall before the elevator. The sadness settles in upon me as I reflect on the losses my friend has endured.

She was a volunteer ministry assistant with me for many years. A relentless chronic illness is gradually sapping her energy and her abilities, and now she is confined to one small room in this extended care facility.

On this visit she told me that the woman in the next room was dying and nobody cared. She also spoke about the wife who comes every day and stays all day to be with and feed her husband. There is no conversation at the meal tables. A disoriented man had tried to break into her room. The person across the hall is sleeping. The sound of labored breathing penetrates the atmosphere and stirs uneasiness when it momentarily stops or is interrupted by choking.

The morning after this latest visit my phone rings early. The call is from my friend in extended care. She tells me that after I left yesterday the social worker had come to do an assessment. After learning of the above report, an offer was made to transfer my friend to another unit. This would be a place where the patients would be higher functioning and she could feel safe. My friend asked if she could have a day to decide as she wanted to talk to me, her pastor, before making this change.

She told me she wondered if she should choose to stay in her current environment. She said she sees the decline in the other patients and knows that is her future, but should she not try to be useful for as long as she had something to give? Shouldn't she stay and find some ways to help? "Maybe I am where God wants me to be?"

I recognized, as I listened, that we were walking on Holy Ground. My friend was choosing a sacrificial lifestyle because of her relationship with Jesus. Her favorite song is "I Surrender All" and this is what I see her doing. She is denying a more comfortable experience for herself in order to respond to this call.

After praying with her, I said, "The safest place you will ever be is in the center of God's will. Knowing you, you will get more energy from serving than from being served."

She said she was hoping I would say that. I told her this was her mission field and we would build a prayer support team for her work.

Our conversation ended with her saying, "This is exciting."

*T*REASURES FROM OUR SHELVES

Many of us are in a season of life where we are looking at the things we have kept on our shelves and finding no reason to keep them. What we at one time valued seems to have lost all significance. While this may be true of much memorabilia, there may be another shelf that warrants our attention.

I have been gifted with some wise-beyond-their-years friends who are known as twenty- somethings and are roughly the age of our grandchildren. One of them wrote the following words to me yesterday in the context of my leading the prayer ministry at our church.

"God does not take light your experience. God has given His Word, from which we learn of him (Bible) and He has also given us the Holy Spirit, and we seek His direction and guidance, He leads us.

You also have such rich experiences in prayer, many of which may have been put on a shelf—"out of sight, out of mind"—nonetheless, they are very valid and can be drawn upon even as you lead and as the ministry progresses... God has already given you the tools needed to lead the prayer and other ministries. He has also given Himself. He is your sure foundation, and He will allow you to lead upon His foundation. I do believe He will amaze you."

As I reflect on these words from my young friend, I have been prompted to take another look at my shelves. I am remembering times when I have encountered God in prayer. These memories strengthen my faith today, and I will be watching for how He will give me opportunity to apply them both in the formal ministry of our church and in the circles of people He allows me to encounter in my daily walk.

What do you have on your shelves? Are there treasures there, rich experiences of prayer, that are out of sight, out of mind for you? Maybe it's time to pull them down and dust them off.

Let's not leave our treasures on our shelves!!!

RUNNING TO JESUS

I've met a friend who is so radiant with the Presence of God that I've asked her to take me with her into a deeper relationship with Him.

Her answer was, "I don't know very much. All I know is to run to Jesus."

That picture has directed my heart to Isaiah 30:15, which says, "Return to me, rest in me, embrace quietness and confident trust." What does returning to God (running to Jesus) look like with *Faith Through Aging Eyes*?

Today I am praying this prayer:

"Oh, Papa God,

Those little feet that ran barefoot on the farm and laughed when they landed in a cow pie were mine running to you.

Those teenage feet that fell in love with you and wanted to die for you on a mission field were mine running to you.

Those young adult feet that decided to cut their own path were mine running from you.

Those bruised and blistered feet that made a U-turn of

repentance a decade later were mine stumbling back to you.

Most of my adult life, I have walked circumspectly in your general direction but I have processed my steps through the grid of my own head. I have moved toward you but seldom have I run.

Now, I want to run. I don't care if I stumble. I don't care how I look. I want to go barefoot again and run to you.

And, Papa, when my physical feet can only shuffle and my steps are slow, I want you to hear the feet of my heart racing towards you.

Then I will fall in your arms and be home.

*D*O YOU KNOW WHY YOU ARE HERE?

To acknowledge that aging is a diminishing experience is easy in the abstract. When it becomes personal, it is much more difficult. I am walking with a friend for whom an extended care facility has become her only choice. She is no longer able to function in the home she loves.

This friend now lives her life from one small room. The bed is the center of attention. A small wardrobe, a bedside cabinet, a dresser that doubles as a TV stand and one chair occupy the rest of the floor space. This arrangement of furniture is an obstacle course for navigating her wheel chair.

While visiting, I leave the comfort of our casual conversation and risk asking what she is really feeling. She said she never realized how hard it would be to lose personal freedom. By this she means that she is not allowed to move from her chair or her bed without pushing a call button and waiting for assistance, which is sometimes slow in coming.

I ask if the staff is competent and kind. My friend says that they are okay, but she has concern that they know so little about her. Every morning they ask her if she knows why she is there. My memory goes back to the days when I worked as a nurse. I suggest to my friend that maybe they are not seeking information for themselves but checking to see if she is aware of where she is and why. I explain that this is a routine question to see if a patient is oriented to time and place.

I wonder if this is one of the reasons God wants me to pray. He really doesn't need me to give Him information. He does want me to be aware of where I am and why.

I'm glad He cares enough to ask me every day, "Do you know why you are here?"

CHECKING MY PULSE

As I was leading our Senior Adult Prayer Retreat the other day, I once again found myself the learner.

I had just played John Michael Talbot's "Sacred Silence" and directed the group to spend five minutes listening to what the Holy Spirit was saying to each of them.

As my eyes scanned the room, I noticed one man, who was nearly 95 years old, with his right arm in the air, his left hand grasping the extended right wrist, and his mouth hanging open. The nurse in me wondered if he was in distress. I watched for signals that would prompt me to intervene but found none.

When we reported on what we had learned during this time of silence, this man said that the Spirit had prompted him to feel his pulse, and reminded him that Jesus was behind that beat. His heart would beat until Jesus called him home.

This man then invited each of us to feel our pulse and be reminded that each beat is by God's grace and under God's control. Life, the gift of God, measured in time by heartbeats and recognized by a man who is near to the heart of God.

CREATED IN HIS IMAGE

We have the stunning account from the early Bible teachings that we are created in the image of God. We know that image is marred because of sin, but we also know that we have been rescued and are being restored. I wonder how we know when either joy or pain is felt because we are image bearers.

Last week when my precious six-year-old adopted granddaughter was getting packed up to leave from her weekly visit with me, she interrupted her gathering of stuff and asked, "Besta, if you are still living when I am grown, can I bring my baby to see you? Will you hold her in your arms by the door like you held me when I was a baby?"

These precious words flooded my heart with joy. I cherished her eye contact as she processed the memory of the story she had been told of how our relationship began. I was honored to be in dreams of life to come. I told her I would love for her to bring her baby.

Was this response on my part a reflection of how God feels when we somehow tell Him that spending time with Him is special and we want our children to experience it, too?

Does being created in His image also mean we share His pain?

My heart is crushed today because my friend is in a deepening trench of unrelenting pain. This pain has such a grip on her that she is rejecting me. I am finding no welcome for my effort to show compassion.

I know that the depth of my pain could be because I don't trust God to undertake for my friend. If this is the case, I need to repent. But is it possible that I am sharing in His sufferings?

Might this be a time when, as the Holy Spirit picks up my inarticulate groaning, my feeble attempts at prayer become a powerful communication between the Spirit within, the Son interceding and the Father attending?

How does being an image-bearer affect my view of both joyful delight and heartbreak?

REALIGNING MY PERISCOPE

I have one area of my life where the Presence of God is blurred.

I know, cognitively, that God is good.

An African greeting begins:

"God is good," followed by the response "All the time."

The greeting goes on:

"All the time," and the response is "God is good."

This is a greeting that feels right and resonates with truth.

When life's circumstances align with it, joy is released.

When life's circumstances blur the footprints of God's goodness, the canvas of faith must be stretched big enough to wrap around unbelief.

I write about this in a rambling, unfocused way because my struggle lacks focus.

As I prayed about this, I started thinking about a periscope. This instrument allows you to look around an obstacle by encasing two mirrors at 45-degree angles at each end of a tube.

The first mirror must be clean and clear in order for the image from the second mirror to be undistorted.

Am I looking at God through the circumstances of my life or am I looking at the circumstances of my life through God?

If my initial mirror is coated with pain and struggle, God does not look good in the second mirror.

If I reverse the periscope and look first at God, and then see my pain and struggle through Him, the circumstances of my life appear strangely dim.

I am not very skilled at realigning my periscope but I do believe there is power in the words of an old hymn, "Turn your eyes upon Jesus, look full in His wonderful face, and the things of earth will grow strangely dim in the light of His glory and grace."

*T*OO MUCH RED INK

It's not hard to remember the sinking feeling that came with getting an assignment back from a teacher and finding it all marked up with red ink. It's not a very long journey from "I got a failing grade" to "I am a failure."

I wonder if on our journey with Jesus we are too quick to grab the pen with red ink. Do we, in our essential task of defending the absolute truth of the gospel, extend this "pen with red ink" to that which may be better left to the illumination of process?

Here is the story that is prompting this question for me:

A lady of retirement age, whom I did not know, came to our home to assist me with a project. As we talked, she revealed to me that she had several precarious health conditions. As I listened, I felt led to ask, "Do you know Jesus?"

"Oh, yes," she replied with evidence of warmth and familiarity. She then went on to tell me about her mother's deathbed experience. It had been a protracted dying, and the family had spent a week at this mother's bedside.

After several assurances from the family that permission was given to die, this mother drew her final breath. As she did, she raised her arms toward heaven, broke into a big smile, and said, "Harold."

The lady telling this story choked up and said that Harold was her father's name. She then spoke to me in an emotional whisper, "I think Harold was the angel God sent to take my mother home to heaven."

I listened and stayed quiet. I was aware that there would have been a time in my own journey where I would have needed to explain that we don't become angels. Somehow, in this story, the blood of Jesus is all the red ink I needed.

THE DOOR WAS ALWAYS OPEN

Tomorrow I am going to the closing on the sale of my Aunt's house. I am the trustee of her estate so I will be the one signing the papers.

Today, her son brought me the keys to this house so I could give them to the new owner.

I was surprised at how strange it felt to have, for the first time in my life, a key to my Aunt's house.

I guess I didn't know she even had a key. The door was always open. I could walk into her house at anytime, unannounced.

I grew up on a farm. We didn't have a key to our house either.

We did have a telephone. It was a party line, and our number was 4F2211. That meant when there were two short rings followed by two long rings, we would answer.

In the old days, no one wasted time on the phone asking if they could come over. They just came.

Now no one goes anywhere without having mutually secured the time in our smart phones.

It will feel like a loss to turn these keys over tomorrow.

It won't be a loss of keys. It will be the loss of a culture where dropping in was not an intrusion. It will be the loss of a community of belonging.

Are doors meant to lock people out or to invite people in?

What was God telling us when He tore the curtain from top to bottom?

I'm glad I have a picture of what an open door looks like.

It will be sad to bring a key to the closing. The key does not fit in the story.

A GOOD DAY TO MOVE

Psalm 91:1 in the Amplified says, *"He who dwells in the secret place of the Most High shall remain stable and fixed under the shadow of the Almighty (Whose power no foe can withstand)."*

When Christ went to the cross, the curtain of the temple was torn in two. This one act, initiated from above, opened the way for those of us who are children of God not only to walk directly into His Presence but to also dwell there.

Most of us who are navigating *Faith Through Aging Eyes* know that we are going to have to move someday. We consider the options of a smaller house, a condo, an apartment, and a senior living center. We hope we won't need to live in a nursing home and worry about having enough money.

I am not discounting the reality and stress of choosing a physical environment that will accommodate the probability of weakness and dependence, but today I want to talk about another kind of move. I want to invite you to consider with me the invitation to dwell in the secret place of the Most High.

This home became accessible to us when the curtain was torn in two.

As I checked some things out, I learned that there is a secret place available for me, and it has actually been reserved in my name for a long time. I was stunned to find out as I read the application that everything has already been paid in full. This includes all amenities. I quickly checked for the length of the contract and saw that it is guaranteed for eternity.

This is a place where I can dwell, even as I wander through the physical options noted above. I wonder why I haven't moved into this secret place before.

Spend some time in Psalm 91 to learn more about His protection and provision. Move in today!

*T*HAT IS WHAT I DO

I recently emailed a request to someone I was just getting to know and risked asking her to guide me in the steps I needed to take for a project that has been a dream of mine.

To my delight, her response was, "That is what I do!"

I have since recognized that this same response is what I often get from God. I bring Him the broken pieces of my story and ask the impossible. I ask Him to fix it. He smiles and says, "That is what I do."

I ask Him to help me understand what part is mine in someone else's broken story. He smiles and says, "That is what I do."

I ask Him to empower me to bring Him glory. He smiles and says, "That is what I do."

I ask Him to forgive me for my unbelief and my careless thoughts. He smiles and says, "That is what I DID."

Then I remember that on this side of the cross, I can pray from victory and not for victory.

I thank Him for reminding me. He smiles and says, "That is what I do."

I WANT TO BE LIKE THAT

We have three services on a Sunday morning and those who attend generally choose the same hour each week, so much so that each service has a personality of its own.

This past weekend one of our senior ladies came in at the very end of the first hour. She got settled in her usual pew just as our senior pastor stood up to close in prayer.

This lady who had just arrived was directly in my line of vision. I watched as she realized what had happened and tried to control her laughter. Her whole body was laughing out loud, but she was trying to do it quietly in respect for the benediction.

I knew she had forgotten to set back her alarm clock to account for daylight savings time.

She didn't know she was teaching me to laugh at myself. To burst into laughter at what could have been a reason for embarrassment confirmed that she takes God very seriously but she has learned not to take herself too seriously.

Is this a blueprint for finishing well?

*T*HE COMFORT OF BEING KNOWN

A long-time friend came with me for a medical procedure today. I invited her into the room where all the questions are asked. It felt good to know that as I responded to inquiries regarding my health history and lifestyle behavior, none of the answers would be a surprise to her.

When the nurse explained to both of us that after my "conscious sedation" I would probably be repetitive and forgetful, my friend and I answered in concert that this would not be different from any other day.

Who knows you and how did it happen?

Do you have anyone with whom you do not need to pretend?

How aware are you that God knows your thoughts before you speak?

Does this give you freedom to talk to Him about anything and everything?

Sometimes we complicate this conversation with God by calling it prayer.

You have searched me, Lord, and you know me. You know when I sit and when I rise; you perceive my thoughts from afar. You discern my going out and my lying down; you are familiar with all my ways. (Psalms 139:1-3 NIV)

WHEN MY HEART IS TOO HEAVY

I'm giving my imagination freedom to stage some potential scenes.

Tonight I am picturing a waiting room full of people who are bringing their stories to Jesus. His office is not a closed-door room but rather a type of stage that enables me to see and hear His interactions with those who have registered ahead of me.

I watch as a mother glowingly tells Him that even though her daughter has lost a leg to cancer, their faith has been strengthened, and their love for Him has deepened.

I listen as a man tells of the return of his son. Tears flow down his face as he recounts the joy of a restored relationship.

I will be next.

I know the story I was hoping to bring. I know the story I was expecting to bring. But the real story is not what I have hoped or expected. I don't know how to reconcile my shattered dreams with what I know of the character of Jesus. I have to decide if I take my turn and walk into His

Presence with my fear and confusion or if I just leave and let someone else go next.

My heart is too heavy to make a decision. I sleep for awhile, and when I awake I look to the stage again. I can't tell what Jesus is doing. He doesn't look like he is paying attention.

The thought crosses my mind that maybe my story is so agonizing because I have misunderstood my assignment. Did I pick up the wrong homework? Have I spent the majority of my life on a project I have crafted for myself?

When my hopes began to fade, did I create in my own mind a "calling" that I have attributed to Him and therefore spiritualized my suffering? I know a jury of peers would look with critical pity on my story and scold me for my unwillingness to recognize my relentless pursuit of a failing endeavor.

I wonder if Jesus will do the same.

I glance at the magazine table beside me. I see the cover page and it says, "Has God really said?" The article questions the promises of God. I try to see who has authored this but cannot as the name is smudged.

I look again at the stage and see Jesus writing something. He hands the note to a messenger who gives it to me. I read, "The enemy is threshing you, but I am praying for you that your faith does not fail."

A MODEL FOR PRAYER

My seven-year-old granddaughter said, "Besta, the Bible you gave me doesn't work in Sunday School."

I asked her to explain. She said that the Bible I had given her was filled with stories and in Sunday school they asked for chapter and verse.

Delighted that she was taking such an interest in the Bible, I told her she could go to the church bookstore and find a Bible that would work in Sunday School. I said that she should pick it out with her mother's help and I would pay for it.

Soon afterwards I got this text "Dear Besta, today I got my Bible. Today is 4/18/14 and I like it because I love Bibles like you. I love you. Please pay me back, Love (name).

I smiled as I read this text and then recognized it as a teaching tool for prayer.

Address the One Who made the promise.

Remind the Promise Maker of today's date.

Remind the Promise Maker that you have done what He asked you to do.

Tell the promise keeper you love Him.

Cash in on the promise.

Choose a promise and claim the benefit of a Resurrected Promise Keeper.

Example: "Lord God, You have promised that you will never leave me. Today is a day that I desperately need to be aware of Your Presence. I have released my cares to you just as you instructed me to do. I love you. So now please show up in my life in a way that I can recognize. In Jesus' name, Amen.

WHAT GOD WANTS FOR ME

This morning a friend prayed that I would embrace what God wants for me as well as what He wants from me. It dovetailed with my reflections on a recent visit from my six-year-old grandchild. This visit was a new experience as it was the first time she took charge of what our activities would be.

She had a myriad of ideas, an authoritative attitude, and an attention span that left us with every venture unfinished.

I spoke to her mom and said I would need to learn what she and Dad were doing for discipline so I could be consistent with it. Her mom responded, "She can do anything she wants at your house."

This is not the answer I expected, but after thinking more about it, I emailed her mother and said I thought her counsel was wise. My grandchild needs a place to just BE and I need someone to just BE WITH.

Here is the mom's response. "Yes, she needs to have a fun, safe and happy relationship with you. At home there are enough rules and regulations. At your house, relationship, safety, trust, and friendship are the most important.

Teaching her about Jesus—vital. And filling her with love, acceptance, and praise is what she needs."

I wrote back, "This assignment fills me with joy. Thank you!"

I basked in the love extended to me by these parents. They are carrying the heavy load of providing a structure at home where their children develop habits of responsibility and respect. At my house, while not negating these goals, we can focus on enjoying our relationship.

How different is this from what God wants for me. Jesus paid the price that grants me relational access to the Father. Today, I believe He wants me to embrace that relationship with joy and trust.

BEING ATTENTIVE TO OUR POSTURE

As I am preparing for a hike, I am reminded that posture is important. As I go for my walk, I try to remember to press my tummy toward my spine, let my shoulders relax and widen, and picture a suction cup on the top of my head pulling me taller.

I can do one of these things easily, but it is awkward to hold all of these positions at the same time. I am working on improving my posture because I believe it will be of benefit when I am challenged on the long hike for which I am becoming prepared.

Is there also a posture that has benefit for spiritual empowerment? St. Augustine said that the proper posture for prayer was standing proud and erect because we no longer have to grovel before God or fear God if God is like Jesus.

I remember my first experience of hearing group prayer in an Asian context. When the leader of a seminar called for prayer, the participants jumped to their feet and begin shouting together in a way that reminded me of what we do in our culture when our team scores a touchdown.

I know there are times to be quiet and on our knees before God.

But maybe we need to be reminded of the power that we have in prayer, the position we hold in Jesus, and then look the part.

*T*HIS CHILD MUST LIVE HERE

Not long ago I was invited to a fellowship group at the home of a friend. As everyone began to respond to his invitation, it became apparent to the friend who had invited me that his home was too small. He quickly made a location change and emailed me the address of where the event would be held.

On the evening of the event, I punched the address into my GPS and started following the directions. As I pulled up to the house, I noticed many cars parked up and down the street. I walked toward the house realizing that not only did I not know who lived there, but I didn't really know the other guests.

I took a seat and, watching with interest, found myself amused and expectant as to how this event would turn out.

There were three little dogs running around inside the home. Most of us kept a cautious distance from these animals but one little girl jumped into the midst of them and started playing with them. I reasoned, "This child must live here."

I wonder what behaviors people pick up when they watch

those of us who say that we are children of our heavenly Father and joint heirs with King Jesus.

Do they see us "at home" in the Presence of God? Do they see us relaxed as we talk about our Provider? Do they see us honoring our Father by working and playing well with each other? Do they see us keeping a cautious distance from risk or do they see us free to enter because we know who and where we are?

Is there any evidence in our life that would even give an angel a clue that we are citizens of heaven?

That this child must live here?

*F*OLLOWING JESUS IS NOT TOO HARD

I listened as these words were spoken with confidence and joy by a charismatic prophet from Macedonia. This man said, "You only think it is hard because someone told you it was hard." I should probably stop right here and let you think about this for a couple of days. I did after I heard it. In my reflection on this statement, I found myself asking this question: "Is following Jesus hard for me because I am not listening well to what He is asking me to do?"

A memory from my childhood on a dairy farm is intriguing to me.

I was probably about nine years old when I first started doing this one "small" but critical task. It happened during haying season. A four-wheeled long-tongued wagon would be driven from the hayfield into our farmyard. The hired man would then come to the door and call for me. It was my responsibility to take the grown man's place on the tractor and back the wagon up the barn bridge so the hay could be unloaded in the hayloft.

The barn bridge, which accessed the top floor of the barn, was secured on one side by a grassy slope and on the other by vertical cement blocks, which produced a twenty-foot drop into the pig pen. The margin for error in backing this heavy-laden four-wheeled long-tongued wagon up this bridge was inches.

My dad trusted me to do it.

For some reason, when Dad had demonstrated to me that in order to accomplish this task I needed to start with the tractor at a specific place at an exact angle, maintaining a consistent speed, I did exactly that. Dad knew how it needed to be done, and it never crossed my mind that I should try an alternative method or question his directions.

I didn't wonder at the time, but I do wonder now, what these men must have felt like, not being trusted to back this wagon up and having to ask a young girl to do it. Dad knew he could trust me.

I knew that when the wagon was on the barn floor, my part of this process was done.

Following Dad was not hard.

How do I complicate following Jesus?

I KNOW MY DADDY

Yesterday I had a day with my granddaughter, who has been eight years old for six days. We planned our day together to include choosing and delivering some small gifts for people who are sick or in nursing homes.

Since her daddy was home with a cold, we included him on our list. I asked, "What can we get for your daddy that would be really special?" My granddaughter quickly answered, "Cherries in a can." Wanting to make sure this would really be a treat, I asked if he would rather have big red cherries with stems. A confident smile confirmed her decision. "I know my daddy," she replied.

It was impossible to miss the impact of this statement.

Looking for ways to apply this to our relationship with our Father in heaven, I asked her, "What needs to happen in order for you to say, 'I know my daddy'?"

The answer she gave included listen to him, spend time with him, watch him, and do things with him.

As I absorbed these answers, I knew they were an invitation for me to celebrate that I also know my "Daddy," more formally called "Our Father in Heaven."

Knowing Him gives me confidence. Knowing Him empowers me to make choices that will please Him. Knowing Him makes me want to bring Him something that will be special for Him today.

*T*HERE IS NO ONE TO ASK

My sister called to ask me if I remember her having chicken pox when she was five years old. One of the realities of being in the top chronological layer of generations is that there is no one left on earth that remembers your childhood. In this case, my sister was trying to decide if she should get the shingles vaccine.

I knew she'd had measles. I knew I did not have measles. I knew I'd had chicken pox. But, did she? I don't know.

As I think about this, somehow I feel like an orphan. There is no one who remembers this important information. There is no one to retell the stories either. Like how I always cut my bread into squares before Mom poured milk and sugar on it. Everyone else in our family tore the bread in pieces and put them in a cup.

This longing for someone to acknowledge the reality of my childhood reflects the teaching of C. S. Lewis that we never stop being a child. He compares our aging to rings on a tree stump. The inner ring representing childhood does not disappear but is wrapped around by increasingly larger rings as decades pass.

I'm glad today that Papa God not only makes room for childlike faith in *Faith Through Aging Eyes* but that He delights in it.

As I long for someone to remember my childhood, remembering that I am still a child turns my longing into gratitude.

Thank you, Papa God, for not forgetting. Thank you that in You I will never be an orphan. Thank you that you remember every detail of my story. Thank you, more importantly, that I have a role to play in your story.

There is Someone to ask.

E'VE BEEN ON A JOURNEY TOGETHER

These words were spoken with precision and passion as my husband's cardiologist honored us by telling us personally of his retirement.

This doctor is an elegant man, both in his appearance and his manner. His presence changes the atmosphere of a room as he brings confidence, calm, and care.

We were not surprised by this announcement as we had sat in the office waiting room, witnessing the tearful hugs and statements of appreciation by those who had earlier appointments. Today he walked each patient out to the desk as he assigned him or her to a younger colleague.

Waiting for him was a given. We knew he would be late because he was giving the same personal attention to the person ahead of us that he would give to us. Once in his office, time seemed to stop. The only thing important to him was the doctor/patient relationship of the moment.

My husband's heart condition has a long, complicated history and a precarious prognosis, but it has never felt like the focus when we met with this doctor.

He seemed more interested in the quality of our life. He asked questions about our ministry as pastors and discussed the vocation of medicine as ministry.

He asked thoughtful questions that would uncover a masked depression or a settling for a more limited life than our condition mandates.

He loved to hear that we did not have a kitchen table because that is where we dance.

On most visits he reminded us that a day without wine is like a day without sunshine. We talked about the risk of wine causing my husband's heart to flutter, and he said that a small glass was okay with him.

After caring for us as people, he attended to my husband's pathology by listening with competence to his heart and lungs. We completely trusted his assurance that all was well. More importantly, we trusted the man who had learned to treat his patients as unique creations made in the image of God. He knows that our bodies are designed for temporary use so he cares for them without challenging their finitude.

Today we had our last appointment with this cardiologist. We will miss these times where dementia was treated with dignity and a diseased heart took second place to a life well lived.

Memories of these office visits will continue to bless us.

We have seen a model of what Jesus may have looked like if God had chosen to visit earth in Waukesha two thousand years later than His appearance in Galilee.

We have been on a journey together.

$\mathcal{S}$TRENGTH THROUGH WHISPERED WEAKNESS

My friend has been in a Surgical Intensive Care Unit for a week.

Her health crisis came without warning. She was awakened at 2 a.m. with symptoms that prompted her family to call 911. The ER transferred her to Surgical Intensive Care, unresponsive with a brain bleed.

This week has heightened the tension between standing firm that God heals and frightening medical data. Those who were interceding for her could have been placed on a continuum. Some were taking authority, claiming healing with bold confidence, others scanning the ICU monitors and reminding God that the ball was in His court.

Hope was fed when she was able to wiggle her feet on command and then hold up two fingers. It looked like she would survive this event, but what neurological damage had been done?

Prior to this hospitalization, I have only known this friend as one whose prayers stir my spirit and whose strength in God is contagious. When I have been privileged to meet personally with her, I have seen myself as a student meeting with a teacher. This is especially true when the conversation is focused on the authority we have as children of God.

This week her physical weakness has jolted me into a place of needing to step up. My heart raced when my phone rang and her name appeared on the caller ID. I could barely hear her as she whispered, "Roselyn, I need you to pray. TAKE AUTHORITY!"

It felt like my math professor was asking me to help solve a problem that he knew we had not covered in class.

Yet, there was no mistaking that my friend was calling me and that she knew from Whom the authority comes.

I prayed. I took authority over this illness in the Name of Jesus. I practiced praying with the confidence I have heard in her as she prayed. I remembered her telling me "Sometimes you have to be violent with the enemy."

It's two weeks now since this medical event occurred. Many prayers and much reason to praise have been recorded. We are watching to see how God will bring glory to Himself, as her healing has been amazing.

I will visit her today and find this friend restored to the person of strength and vitality I had come to know. She texted last night that she was planning a "jail break," signifying she has been in the hospital long enough.

As I continue to process all that has transpired, I want to embrace a heart of gratitude that never forgets that His strength is made perfect in weakness.

In her weakness she knew that authority needed to be taken in the name of Jesus. In my weakness, I recognized that the power to take authority is available to me.

*A*LL OF A SUDDEN IT CREPT UP

I was reviewing life with a Senior Adult couple in our church lobby recently. As they told of their granddaughter's plan to spend time in Spain, I said, "That will give you a place to visit."

They both shook their heads and together said that they had gotten old. "All of a sudden it crept up," the wife explained. As my friend made this statement, she caught the incongruity. "How can something like that be?" she mused.

Her husband tried to help by saying it was like "Jumbo Shrimp" but that didn't really help.

Aging both stuns us with its suddenness and lulls us with its subtleness. I really don't look in the mirror very often because I would rather picture myself at the age I feel rather than the age I look to others.

But maybe both views are important. Being able to think of myself as young is held in tension with the reality of my years. It allows me to dream about all the things I still want to do even as I prepare for the day when I will need to let others do for me.

I pray that I can look through this bifocal lens with faith because all of a sudden it will creep up. Where are you on your journey toward becoming an older person?

AN OFFICE VISIT

The couple was newlyweds, even though age qualified them for Medicare. It was a routine physical for the husband, and his wife accompanied him with pad and pen in hand.

This was a second marriage for the husband. His first wife of 35 years had died three years earlier. This man's first wife and his current new wife had been friends for years and shared much, including personal information regarding the husband's health and habits.

As the doctor began his physical examination, the wife interrupted by saying, "He doesn't hear well now, and his first wife said he didn't hear well then."

Without a pause in his routine or an acknowledgment of the concern, the doctor asked the husband, "Other than marital deafness, how is your hearing?"

Are we learning to laugh at ourselves?

BUT SHE LOVED JESUS

I wasn't prepared for the story I would hear when I called to check up on this senior adult friend. She lives in senior housing and usually attends our meetings, but I hadn't seen her in a couple of weeks.

"Oh, I'm just tired," she said. "I have new medicine for my heart and it drains me of my energy." She quickly changed the subject and said, "You will never believe what happened this week."

I settled in to listen to the story.

She said, "You know for our Bible Study here we have a plan where those of us who live alone call each other every day to make sure we are okay."

I interrupted and asked, "Are you able to go to the Bible Studies?"

"Yes," she answered. "I lead them." Eager to get to her story, she continued. "This week the person assigned to call J didn't get an answer. So the next step was to call me and I tried to call J. Still no answer. I then contacted the building manager, and after getting no response at J's door, he opened it and we walked in together."

My friend started laughing as she said, "Guess what we found?"

Before I could respond she said, still laughing, "J was dead in bed."

Trying to reconcile the words I was hearing with the joyful delivery, I asked, "Is this your highlight of the week? Finding your friend dead in bed?"

"But Roselyn," she quickly explained, "J loved Jesus."

She commented further, "Everything in her apartment was in its place. It looked like she was planning a trip." Laughing again my friend said, "I have so much stuff in my apartment that when my turn comes, my daughter will need a road map to find me."

When death can be embraced as a part of life, the impact is softened. Knowing the one who died loved Jesus enables a memorial service to be a celebration of life. We grieve, but not as those who have no hope!

DEFAULT SETTING

What does the word "default" really mean? In the English language, "default" can be used in many different ways, but the definition I want to explore here is the meaning when a technician says your computer or phone operates a certain way because of the default setting. This is what I learned.

Default is the option that is selected automatically unless an alternative is specified. If this is possible with technology, could I also create some default settings in my heart?

When I find myself the recipient of disappointment, do I default to trust? Or do I need to take the long road with stops at the village of doubting the goodness of God? Do I visit the city of battling God for control or the continent of immobilizing fear?

I remember the time I was learning to play tennis. I did great for my first two lessons and not so great on my third. I told my instructor I thought I was getting worse instead of better. She replied that she was just serving me harder shots to return.

There is no denying that when God gives us the gift of a long life, it comes with some pretty tough return shots.

DEFAULT SETTING

This book is titled *Faith Through Aging Eyes*, and I wonder if the confession of the aging person needs to be that the battle intensifies and sometimes we resort to a default setting from exhaustion.

What are you doing to make trust your default setting?

*D*ID YOU CALL A WRONG NUMBER?

I answered my phone and learned the call was from a nurse calling on behalf of my health insurance company. She said she wanted to go over some information with me that would help me with prevention strategies. Her first recommendation was that I not stand up too fast. She said if I did, my blood pressure would drop, I would probably faint, and then could break a bone.

Did she call the wrong number or does she really think I am at risk for this event?

Then she asked if I could see. She wondered if I had had my eyes tested for glaucoma. If I did that preventatively, it could keep me from going blind.

Did she call the wrong number or does she think I am at risk for this?

She concluded by asking if I had had a colonoscopy in the last ten years. I told her that I had a prescription for one but I hadn't had time to enjoy it. She encouraged me to do it before it is too late.

Did she call the wrong number or does she think…?

DID YOU CALL A WRONG NUMBER?

Oh, no! Do you think the insurance company checked my date of birth?

*D*OES GOD ANSWER PRAYERS RANDOMLY?

A week ago I received a prayer request from a friend who is a doctor in northern India. It happened that her email came through at 4:18 a.m. I woke up at just that time and heard the signal that let me know I had a message.

I read the request, quickly wrote my prayer for her and clicked reply. I prayed that the fog would lift so the trains could maintain their schedules, that there would be protection from the cold, that her arthritic hands would be free from pain, and that her ministry to her dying patients would be anointed by the Holy Spirit.

She replied with great gratitude for my prayer. The fog had indeed lifted. The train schedules were manageable. Her hands were pain-free, and she was able to minister with power.

I read this reply in the home of my friend for whom I have prayed for decades, but whose pain is unrelenting, and I asked God, "Why do you answer some prayers and not others?"

He replied, "I answer them all."

The testimonies we are most comfortable giving and hearing are those where God's footprints are easily tracked.

We like instant answers.

Thankfully, when we find ourselves with the challenge of believing without the benefit of tangible evidence, scripture reminds us we are not the first believers to be trusted with what appears to be a silent God.

A dramatic example is the story of John, Jesus' close friend, standing at the foot of the cross watching Jesus being crucified.

What would his answer be to, "Does God answer prayer?" on the Friday Jesus died. How would that answer change three days later?

Let's remember on what side of the cross we stand! When we have the proper perspective, we can say, "Yes, Lord, you do answer them all."

*F*INDING A NEW RHYTHM

Life has a way of interrupting a familiar rhythm and demanding an accommodation to a new beat.

It happens with piano lessons, too. Just as you get comfortable with the assigned music, there is a numerical sign that lets you know that the next measure will have a new rhythm.

In life it happens with a death, the loss of a job, the birth of a child, a broken relationship, or the burning down of a house.

I am finding myself seeking to adapt to a new rhythm. I didn't choose this change, but since it has happened, I am looking for ways to hang it in the best possible light. I am asking myself what is important to do every day. Who do I want in my inner circle of relationships? Would someone watching my life know what I value?

I've been reading in the book of Mark, searching for the rhythm Jesus modeled. He deliberately sought solitude, time with His Father, time with His friends, responded with compassion by the interruption of a sick person, and set some boundaries for the overwhelming crowds. He heard a beat that governed His life.

May we listen to this beat and quickly respond. Then we too can say "It is finished" when there is still much to do.

*W*HAT'S YOUR ANSWER

I have a friendship that I deeply cherish even though we only connect once every two years and then for just a few hours yet that brief time consistently nurtures my soul and empowers me to travel light.

We both agree that our times together are God-encounters. One of the reasons we know this is that each of us feels as though we are the needy one coming to the other for help.

We had a precious morning together this week.

I told him how disappointed I was in an area of my life where I acknowledge the call of God, respond with obedience, and embrace His promises but still battle terror.

His response initially appeared to be one where he hadn't even heard me. He started telling me a story that didn't seem to have any connection to my struggle.

This story was his memory of being drafted by the army to go to Vietnam. The prospect was one for which he was not physically, emotionally, or spiritually prepared. He just couldn't fathom being in that environment and potentially using a weapon.

Desperate, he sought help from his pastor. After hearing all the reasons that this assignment was totally impossible for him to fulfill, the pastor asked, "If God asked you to go to Vietnam and die, would you go?" My friend tried to reason with his pastor, but the question remained the same.

Finally, this friend said, "Yes."

"Well then," the pastor replied, "That's your answer."

And like a motion-sensitive floodlight penetrating the darkness, I knew this was my answer, too.

RESTING IN THE SECOND STORY

One of the benefits of *Faith Through Aging Eyes* is the realization that I have been cast for two movies that are playing simultaneously.

The first movie depicts the ordinary events of life. My role in this is obvious to anyone who watches. I do things like eat, sleep, meet with friends, read, pay bills, and feed my cat.

The second movie is revealed by grace through faith. When the curtain lifts, allowing me to view this story behind the story, it always prompts worship.

An illustration of this is a phone call I made to a missionary who was home on furlough. My reason for calling was to see if she knew of a project that we could support with donations from a Senior Adult Worship Service. When I asked the question, this missionary burst into tears. At the very moment, this missionary was looking out the window praying for a way to buy rice for some starving refugees.

Another window into the second story happened when I needed to suspend my Camino walk because of a painful knee. It "just so happened" that a 22-year-old girl on this same pilgrimage also had a painful knee and, thankfully, access to a car. We arranged to meet up with our hiking group at the next destination but because the two of us would arrive much sooner, we simply stayed at our current hotel and talked.

As we were discussing the book she was reading, which just happened to be a Bible, she recognized that God wanted a relationship with her. The curtain to the second story opened as I realized that the painful knee from the first story was a window into my young friend's encounter with God.

When this happens often enough, one becomes convinced that there are always two stories being played out. One is our ordinary life, while the other gives us glimpses into what God is doing. In the first, much seems random and mundane. In the second, although we only catch glimpses, we recognize the sovereignty of God.

Psalm 91 invites us to live in the second story. The name given to this area of real estate is the "Secret Place of the Most High." Those who live there engage in "hosting the presence of God."

God is always sending us invitations to rest in the second story. It happens when a verse you are studying in your Bible jumps off the page and you know it is His Word personally given to you. It happens when He speaks to you in prayer or when something He created opens your eyes to the character of the Creator. It happens when someone who is already resting in the second story prompts you to ask if there is room for one more.

I want to learn to rest in the second story.

*F*INDING JESUS IN A PLACE LIKE THIS

The conception of these thoughts rests in a question that has been burned indelibly into my heart.

My friend was slowly regaining consciousness as she was recovering from a life-threatening brain bleed. She was able to raise two fingers on command. To my delight, as I stood beside her SICU bed, she looked at me with recognition and asked, "How do you find Jesus in a place like this?"

I knew the place she was referencing was not the hospital room but rather the mental wilderness of not being able to access her own mind.

My answer, which seems weak in hindsight, was "You rest and let others pray for you."

Since this memorable day, I have pondered the various encounters we have with "a place like this," where finding Jesus feels elusive.

Maybe the "place" is a physical or mental health crisis, maybe it is a relational crash, maybe it is a dashed hope, or a mountain that refuses to move.

All of these present the potential for a failure of faith. I am going to risk saying each of us have our personal "place."

I am in one today. As I was looking for Jesus, my phone rang. I answered and decided not to say the expected "fine" when asked how I was doing. Instead, I said I was struggling.

The person immediately said, "I will pray for you" and then did so with reference to identity and authority. I allowed her prayer to transfer my dilemma to the arms of Jesus. As she prayed, I was able to exchange the yoke that was choking me to the one in which He carries the heavy load.

We took comfort in the promise that when two agree in prayer, the answer is on the way. We acknowledged the precise timing of this phone call to me.

I don't have an easy answer for how to find Jesus in "a place like this," but the scenario feels less desperate.

Maybe finding Jesus is not that elusive. Maybe Jesus was never lost!

*T*HE GIFT OF "NO CONTROL"

It's hard for me to let go of the delusion that I have some control. I try to defend this lie by setting up trust accounts, investing in life insurance and establishing safeguards. But God, in His faithfulness, is relentless in tearing down these fragile structures from which I try to extract a mindset of confidence and peace.

This journey of *Faith Through Aging Eyes* is faithful in providing experiences where trusting God is the only option. The diminishing of aging in itself erodes the illusion of control.

Our own bodies do not respond in the way we have learned to expect. Our circle of family and friends are in transition. We find ourselves deleting more contacts than we add. Those we have leaned on have limited power to keep their promises, much as they would like to.

All of this, and much more, is designed to lead us to a reality of dependence.

A friend recently asked me, "How much control do you really have?"

I wanted her question to be rhetorical but she waited patiently until I answered, "None."

I am learning to believe it.

I wonder if *Faith Through Aging Eyes* empowers us to embrace loss of control as a gift rather than a lament.

What do we have to know about God in order to celebrate the gift of no control?

I DIDN'T CALL FOR ANY REASON

My phone rang. As I picked it up, I recognized the caller as my nephew. The physical distance between us prohibits meeting for coffee.

I said "Hello" and he responded with "Hello."

This was followed by silence.

I asked how he was doing, and he said he was doing fine.

This was followed by silence.

I then asked if he'd called for any reason.

"No," he responded.

I carried the conversation from that time on. We didn't talk about anything that seemed important, but my heart was singing as we simply connected. My nephew simply wanted to talk and I was honored.

I wonder if God would like us to pray from that model. I know He welcomes us when we call to thank Him, when we cry out for help, and when we ask for guidance.

But maybe He would love to just hear me say "Hello" and then let Him carry the conversation.

In Isaiah 50:4 we read this: *"The Sovereign Lord has given me a well-instructed tongue, to know the word that sustains the weary. He wakens me morning by morning, wakens my ear to listen like one being instructed."*

I think tomorrow morning I am going to say "Good morning" to God and then listen. If He asks if there is anything He can do for me, I will say I just want to hear His voice.

Have you ever prayed for no reason?

OH, MR. TENTMAKER

It was nice living in this tent when it was strong and secure and the sun was shining and the air was warm.

But, Mr. Tentmaker, it's scary now.

My tent is acting like it's not going to hold together. The poles seem weak and they shift with the wind; a couple of the stakes have wriggled loose from the sand, and worst of all, the canvas has a rip. It no longer protects me from beating rains or stinging flies.

It's scary in here, Mr. Tentmaker. Last week I was sent to the repair shop and some repairman tried to patch the rip in my canvas. It didn't help much though, because the patch pulled away from the edges, and now the tear is worse.

What troubled me most, Mr. Tentmaker, is that the repairmen didn't seem to notice that I was still in the tent. They just worked on the canvas while I shivered inside. I cried out once, but no one seemed to hear me.

I guess my real question is this: "Why did you give me such a flimsy tent?" I can see by looking around the campground that some tents are much stronger and more stable than mine. Why, Mr. Tentmaker, did you pick a tent of such poor quality for me, and even more importantly, what do you intend to do about it?"

"Oh, little tent dweller, as the Creator and Provider of tents, I know all about you and your tent and I love you both.

"I made a tent for myself once and lived in it on your campground. My tent was vulnerable too, and some vicious attackers ripped it to pieces while I was still in it. It was a terrible experience, but you'll be glad to know they couldn't hurt me. In fact, the whole occurrence was a tremendous advantage because it is this very victory over my enemy that frees me to be of present help to you.

"Little tent dweller, I am now prepared to come and live in your tent with you, *if you will invite me.* As we dwell together, you will learn that real security comes from my being in your tent with you. When the storms come, you can huddle in my arms, and I'll hold you. When the canvas rips, we'll go to the repair shop together.

"Someday, little tent dweller, your tent will collapse, for I've only designed it for temporary use. When it does, you and I will leave this tent together. I promise not to leave before you do. Then, free of all that hinders and restricts, we'll move to our permanent home and *being together forever* we will rejoice and be glad."

Therefore we do not lose heart. Though outwardly we are wasting away, yet inwardly we are being renewed day by day. For our light and momentary troubles are achieving for us an eternal glory that far outweighs them all. So we fix our eyes not on what is seen, but on what is unseen, since what is seen is temporary, but what is unseen is eternal.

For we know that if the earthly tent we live in is destroyed, we have a building from God, an eternal house in heaven, not built by human hands. Meanwhile we groan, longing to be clothed instead with our heavenly dwelling, because when we are clothed, we will not be found naked. For while we are in this tent, we groan and are burdened, because we do not wish to be unclothed but to be clothed instead with our heavenly dwelling, so that what is mortal may be swallowed up by life. Now the one who has fashioned us for this very purpose is God, who has given us the Spirit as a deposit, guaranteeing what is to come.

Therefore we are always confident and know that as long as we are at home in the body we are away from the Lord. For we live by faith, not by sight. We are confident, I say, and would prefer to be away from the body and at home with the Lord. So we make it our goal to please him, whether we are at home in the body or away from it.

(2 Corinthians 4:16–5:9 NIV)

Made in the USA
San Bernardino, CA
05 January 2017